W9-BNH-796

The Alexandria Small Business Development Center
1775-B Duke Street
Alexandria VA 22314
(703) 299-9146

PLEASE RETURN TO:

Priced To Sell

The Complete Guide to More Profitable Pricing

HERMAN HOLTZ

UPSTART
PUBLISHING COMPANY
Specializing in Small Business Publishing
a division of Dearborn Publishing Group, Inc.

This publication is designed to provide accurate and authoritative information in regard to the subject matter covered. It is sold with the understanding that the publisher is not engaged in rendering legal, accounting or other professional service. If legal advice or other expert assistance is required, the services of a competent professional person should be sought.

Executive Editor: Bobbye Middendorf
Managing Editor: Jack Kiburz
Interior Design: Lucy Jenkins
Cover Design: The Publishing Services Group

Published by Upstart Publishing Company,
a division of Dearborn Publishing Group, Inc.

Printed in the United States of America

96 97 98   10 9 8 7 6 5 4 3 2 1

Library of Congress Cataloging-in-Publication Data

Holtz, Herman.
    Priced to sell : the complete guide to more profitable pricing / Herman Holtz.
      p.   cm.
    Includes index.
    ISBN 0-936894-92-X (cloth)
    1. Pricing. 2. Service industries—Prices—United States.
  I. Title.
HF5416.5.H65   1996
658.8'16—dc20   95-42325
                                               CIP

Contents

Preface

A major consideration in business from both the proprietor's and customer's viewpoints is and has always been price. Often, it is *the* major factor, beside which every other consideration pales. It is the immediate indicator of value claimed by the seller and is the apparent index to value as perceived by most customers. Some customers always do comparison shopping to find the lowest prices for what they want and generally buy wherever they are able to get the lowest price. Some customers are not seeking the lowest prices but are in quest of other features. And some customers are attracted by the highest prices, regarding these as evidence of quality and, perhaps, of exclusivity. They may actually mistrust the lowest prices. Finally, a few customers never or rarely do comparison shopping, relying on other means for deciding where and what they will buy, perhaps on the recommendation of friends, the blandishments of TV commercials or the lure of yet another "special sale."

Whichever the case, price is necessarily a consideration of the seller and almost always at least one consideration of the customer. In fact, price-setting is often the most difficult matter for the service proprietor to address. While there is the understandable desire to maximize sales, there is a conflicting desire to turn the maximum profit on sales. The two considerations conflict because it is a general assumption that the choice is between great sales volume at small markup and less sales volume at high markup.

One might assume that "priced to sell" immediately implies bargain prices, the maximum number of sales at the minimum markup. Indeed, there is lots of evidence that many business owners do, indeed, operate on that premise. There is, however, good evidence that pricing to sell does not necessarily mean that one must accept razor-thin margins of profit. Ample evidence demonstrates that those offering the lowest prices do not necessarily achieve the highest sales volume because there are many other factors involved. Still, the problem of how to price for best results continues to puzzle even owners who have been in business for years.

The problem becomes most acute in businesses based on a custom service, whether a product is also involved or not. In such a business, the proprietor does not have the help of a manufacturer's list of suggested prices for what the business sells, and it is not easy to determine what "the market" price is for the service—what the common range of prices charged by competitors is. The proprietor may or may not establish his or her own list—for resume writing or research services, for example—but each job is unique in some way, maximizing the number of variables. The market is thus never easy to judge, even on an approximate basis.

Two changes have come about in recent times that convinced me of the need for this book:

1. We are in a high-tech age, trending toward a business society based on service industries. Manufacturing products has been more and more de-emphasized.

2. We are seeing the growth of small businesses and a return to cottage industries in modern dress—home-based businesses making use of and often based on the spawning technologies of today.

There is a connection between these factors. The technologies that spurred the change to a service economy have enabled the smallest businesses to enjoy capabilities once affordable only by large corporations: The smallest business, even the home-based business with a single employee, is likely now to have a computer, a copier, a fax machine, voice mail and other assets that furnish seedbeds for small businesses and enable them to undertake projects and address markets that they could not otherwise target with any hope for success.

There is a great need for pricing information targeted to this growing market of small service business owners, freelancers and consultants. In these pages, we will explore how you can maximize sales and the profitability of those sales; the kinds of rates you can and should get, as well as how to get them—i.e., how to maximize the value of what you do so as to justify top rates for your work. We will examine how customers reason, what motivates them and how to foster that motivation in your customers. Setting high rates for your work is easy enough, but getting those rates—persuading customers to pay them—is another matter, a matter critical to the success of your business. We will address all these issues and offer the key resources and guidance you need to price your services— and then get your price!

Herman Holtz
Silver Spring, Maryland

Chapter 1

Setting the Right Price Will Lead to Success

*"The right price" is often used idiomatically, and some-
what jocularly, to mean an outrageously high, even an
impossibly high price. The most profitable price, however, may or may not be the highest price: It is the one
that is right for your business in the long run.*

In the United States, we have always enjoyed a hospitable climate
for the launching of new, independent enterprises. However, today
the stimulus is greater than ever, and the variety of services is vast
and still expanding.

Mapping Out the Service Sector

Here are just a few of the many services small businesses commonly offer today that one can provide with small investment:

- Information brokering
- Word processing

1

- Public relations
- Technical writing
- Resume writing
- Transcription and word processing
- Video production
- Computer repair
- Consulting
- Advertising
- Copywriting
- General writing and editing
- Computer programming
- Desktop publishing
- Mailing list management
- Contract labor

These are general terms of description, and some of these businesses involve service only, while others produce something or include the provision of some product. Some practitioners generalize in the service they offer, while others specialize. Writers, for example, are almost compelled to specialize because it is difficult to keep up with, much less market to, all the different areas. Thus, there are speech writers, direct mail writers, advertising copywriters, proposal writers, newsletter specialists, technical writers and still others. Nor do they all identify themselves as writers. Some freelancing technical writers call themselves "documentation consultants," for example, and I often sold my own writing services as a proposal consultant. Specialization applies to many other fields.

All of this tends to create a rather complex set of markets and influences. It is therefore not too surprising that a large number of individuals who launch such service businesses grope about uncertainly trying to set their service rates. Operators of newly launched ventures tend to be fearful, on the one hand, that their prices will be too high and that high prices will make it difficult for them to win clients. On the other hand, they fear setting their rates too low. (Some never learn that too low a price can drive some clients away even more swiftly than too high a price.)

Here are just a few such appeals that have appeared in online communications:

> I'm new to consulting and on my first contract. I am currently salaried. I'm thinking about going to an hourly rate and paying my own benefits. How much more than my current rate should I ask just to break even? What should I ask as an hourly rate?

> Should I tell the person that I will base my fee on his specs?

> Should I attempt to swing a "retainer" type deal, getting them to give me a fixed monthly (annual) fee?

> How much do I charge to do this stuff, moonlighting, 1099 basis?

> When I was there, we regularly hired consultants in the $75–$125 range. Should I ask more?

Appealing to others for advice, new entrepreneurs are given widely varying suggestions. One recommendation I have heard too often suggests that they decide how much they wish to earn and then develop a formula for setting rates to yield such an income. Would that it were that easy to set one's income wherever one would like it to be!

Obviously, there are factors beyond your control, and you are not free to arbitrarily set your rates as high as you wish. Still, you can name your price in business, within certain limits. Within those limits you can decide what is the top dollar you can command for your services. The limits are rather broad, however, and you set them yourself, once you determine what the limits are and what your marketing and operating strategies are.

When I was a kid in high school, I had the choice of taking the bus to school—I was given bus fare—or walking the two miles and being able to spend the bus fare on a goody or two. I wasn't especially fond of walking, at least not on a chilly winter morning, but the contemplation of a hot dog or ice cream from one of the many vendors at the school's curbside induced me to walk most mornings. My decision was based on my assessment of the benefits to me, and I "voted" for my personal interests.

Clients always "vote" for their personal interests, as they perceive those interests. There are Fifth Avenue customers (e.g., "carriage trade"), and there are Second Avenue customers ("bargain-basement trade"). The difference between these is not entirely one of economic status. Many people who can easily afford Fifth Avenue prices prefer to shop on Second Avenue, while others think it demeaning to shop for bargains and mistrust any goods that do not cost them Fifth Avenue prices. It is equally true that many working-class people, people of relatively limited means, have Fifth Avenue tastes and psyches and also shy away from bargain prices.

None of this means you can get any price you want simply by demanding it, nor does it suggest that you ought to gouge your customers. Quite the contrary, the general philosophy here is that you can get top-dollar—maximum—rates if you *earn* top-dollar rates by delivering to your clients services they agree justify those rates.

To at least some degree, you are bound by whatever rates are typical and accepted as a de facto standard, but even these can vary widely. They can vary widely according to various factors, such as the nature of the specialty itself, the persuasiveness of your advertising and promotion, and the market. But the market itself may vary, according to the kind of market (kind of customer, that is), the geographic location of the market, the qualifications or credentials of the offeror, and sometimes to transient conditions, such as the abundance or scarcity of qualified suppliers. Here, to illustrate some of this, are just a few sample items abstracted from a rather exhaustive survey carried out by author Janet Ruhl in research for her excellent book, *The Computer Consultant's Guide*

(John Wiley & Sons, Inc., 1994), and who was kind enough to permit me to use a small portion of her data.

Specialty	Location	Rate per Hour	Qualifications
Analysis, Government	DC	$ 60	MBA/CPA
Analysis, Insurance	NJ	100	MBA/CPA
Analysis, Manufacturing	NJ	80	MBA/CPA
Business Analyst	DC	60–80	CPA
Cobol/Mainframe	NYC	(on-site 50)	
Cobol Programming	DC	80–100	

Reprinted by courtesy of Janet Ruhl

Again, writer/publisher Bob Bly, in his monograph on fees, *How to Set Your Fees . . . and Get Paid What You're Worth* (self-published, 1990), suggests varying prices for a variety of writing tasks and services, of which the following is a small sample:

Print advertisement .... $600–$1,500
Sales letter... $750–$2,500
Press release, 1–2 pages........................... $300–$500
Consultation fee... $125/hour
Copy critique and analysis....................... $200–$600

Reprinted by courtesy of Bob Bly

"Me-Too" Business Enterprises

Some businesses are of the "me-too" variety. They offer what all the others in the same business, their competitors, offer, and are all but indistinguishable from their competitors. What they offer is similar as is how they offer it—their advertising or public notices. The proprietors of such businesses hope to somehow capture a large enough share of the market to pay their bills and earn a living just by being available and ready to supply anyone who approaches and wants what they have to sell. In fact, small stores often open next to their largest competitors and live off the overflow of customers, the traffic created by the large store.

Me-too businesses tend to be very much at the mercy of chance and circumstance. As such a business, you may rely simply on being in a well-trafficked milieu so that fortune favors you via the probability statistics: If the demand for your kind of services is great enough—i.e., if there are enough people looking to buy the kind of services you offer and you are able to somehow make all or nearly all of them aware of your existence and the availability of your services—you are likely to win some share of the business.

If you are in a retail front and rely on walk-in trade, location is probably the main critical element in determining how much traffic exists. If you rely on mail or telephone contact, the main critical element is the effectiveness of your advertising—Yellow Pages, circulars, direct mail, print ads and broadcast commercials. If you rely on sales via channels of distribution, which is possible even in a service business, the main critical element is the effectiveness of your distributors and dealers.

Location Is a Factor

The sages of retail businesses, businesses that rely primarily on customers visiting their places of business, are fond of saying that there are three rules for success: location, location and location. That's true for many retail enterprises—shoe stores and restaurants, for example, although there are exceptions. For example, three restaurants failed at a location with which I am familiar, but a fourth restaurant succeeded there.

For some service businesses, location is certainly a factor. If you operate a service that requires customers to come to your premises, location is almost as much a factor as it is to a shoe store or grocery. But even if you contact customers by telephone and mail or go directly to your customers to deliver your service, you must still think about "location" in your marketing plan. That is, you have to consider where and how prospective customers learn of your existence, what you offer and how they can get in touch with you. Your "location," in that sense, may be in the Yellow Pages, in the daily newspaper, in the morning mail or in some other medium that makes you and your business visible. If you are in the Yellow Pages, surrounded by a dozen or more competitors offering similar services, you may depend on that same spillover effect that the shoe store next to the big department store relies on. Something of the location and spillover effect is thus a factor in all businesses, even the home-based.

The Paradox of Competition and Markets

Obviously, you are going to see yourself surrounded by competition, and it is an almost reflex reaction to wish that there were no competition or, at least, much less competition. Ironically enough, that is something of a death wish: In fact, the existence of competition is an asset, not a handicap, to the small business. It is the cumulative effect of marketing effort by many that creates the market. If you had the only resume-writing service in the world, not many job-seekers would know even that such a service was available, much less where to seek it out.

That is even more true in the case of retail stores. Visit 47th Street in New York City, known sometimes as "diamond row" because the majority of stores there are those of diamond merchants and jewelers. The competition is thus intense, of course, but one may safely assume that prospective customers visiting the street are virtually all interested in gemstones. Thus, one may open a store there because the traffic—and the market—exists there.

That is a common situation and is characteristic of the me-too business. The philosophy is simple: My competitors are making a living, so if I do what they do and do it where they do it, I ought to be able to make a living at it too.

On the other hand, to do it differently than your competitors do it, and to be located elsewhere than your competitors are (if theirs is a business that creates a "jewelers' row," a "clothiers' row" or some analogous avenue), is to invite risk. One must consider that other side of the coin, and the majority prefer to do what they believe is playing it safe: doing what competitors are doing.

Not to say that me-too businesses do not succeed. Many do, and some even succeed on a grand scale. Some are in almost-can't-fail enterprises, such as copy shops, print shops and the top fast-food franchises. Relatively few of these have failed, unlike the high-failure businesses, such as full-service restaurants and appliance dealerships. But many small businesses survive in such circumstances by being cautious, carefully managing expenses and keeping risks at a minimum, trading the prospects of growth for maximum protection of their assets. Thus, it is possible to manage survival in business without doing a great deal of marketing, and a great many small businesses do so manage. To some degree, as some pundit has put it, a large part of success in most things results simply from "showing up."

"We're-Different" Business Enterprises

In direct contrast to the me-too business idea, a great many businesses are of the "we're-different" variety. They try to be somehow distinctive, different from, more attractive than and more appealing to their prospective customers than their competitors. As that kind of entrepreneur, you are far less reactive to chance and far more proactive, exploiting opportunities and constantly seeking to create new opportunities. You will push hard to stand out by intensive and innovative promotions, shouting loudly and waving inducements.

Innovation often means risk, but not all innovations add risk. The late Joe Karbo, who made a huge success of the last promotion he conceived before his death, was an innovator. For that last promotion, a little book he wrote and sold as *The Lazy Man's Way to Riches,* Karbo had two innovative ideas, soon copied by others. One was the very idea, still used by many, of telling his tale of woe—bankruptcy, eviction, repossession of his decrepit old automobile, and many other lamentations—and how he suddenly made a brilliant discovery that made him wealthy beyond his dreams, a discovery he would reveal to anyone who sent him $10 for his little book. That was a somewhat risky idea, although Karbo explained later that the only real risk was the money he spent for the first advertisement to test the idea. The other innovation, which aroused much admiration and was widely emulated, did not add risk. In fact, it was intended to reduce the risk, and apparently it did that very well: To support his statements of former poverty and new-found wealth, Karbo included in his full-page advertisement an official-looking certificate signed by his accountant certifying that all the statements and representations he made in his advertisement were true.

The little paperback book Karbo sold was about 70 pages in length and contained no great revelations. It did have some useful information and much drumbeating for Karbo's own version of positive thinking, which he called "dyno-psych." It was reported that Karbo sold over 600,000 copies of that book for $10 each.

There are many ways to be different, or at least to appear to be different. Often, and increasingly today in a tightened economy, the critical element or distinguishing characteristic of many businesses is price, low or discount price. Discounting has become a popular method of retailing in recent years. Many successful businesses, large and small, have been built and perpetuated on that basis. But the reverse is also true: Many businesses have been built and perpetuated on the basis of getting top dollar. Yes, a reputation for being expensive can be bad for business, but it can also be good as an inducement that attracts profitable trade. The high-priced, "exclusive" shop is a distinctive one too.

Examples exist in abundance at both extremes of price. There are certain customers willing and even eager to pay top dollar for what they want and are suspicious of anything priced below their expectations or below their competitors' advertised prices. On the other hand, there are customers who seek almost endlessly for what they want at the lowest possible prices. They are, of course, different customers in any given case. The two appeals are opposed to each other, and it is quite difficult to appeal to both kinds of customer. (Some department stores manage to do this by having bargain basements, where items are priced much lower than those on the upper floors, but those are much like separate businesses.) You must justify your prices, whether you are at one extreme or the other. If you claim low, discount prices, your prices are much more believable if you justify them by such rationales as explaining that you use "plain, pipe-rack fixtures," as Robert Hall did for their clothing stores or, if you are pricing at the other extreme, finding some means for justifying your high prices. Today's customer is relatively sophisticated and won't easily accept unsupported claims.

Probably the business takes on the personality of its owner. Where the me-too business owner tends strongly to avoid risk, the we're-different business owner is likely to be a risk-taker, highly ambitious and intent on doing volume business and growing. Where a risk-taker buys out a me-too business, the business is soon likely to change and take on entirely different characteristics. Of course, the opposite is true also.

(In practice, there is also the middle-road customer, one who is suspicious of both unusually high and unusually low prices and is more likely to pay list prices or sale prices in the traditional middle-class setting than to succumb to the sales arguments of either extreme. A great many businesses survive by appealing primarily to this customer. They probably tend to be far more the me-too kind of business than the we're-different type.)

All kinds of customers are different than other kinds, with respect to a single business or kind of business. Therefore, the business must be structured to pursue a given type of customer. But people are not consistent: There are individuals who can be more than one type of customer, according to individual situations and circumstances. The individual who stubbornly seeks out the lowest price for a pair of jeans or a toothbrush may be interested in only the highest priced jacket or automobile. There are customers for the costly gourmet foods of Sutton Place, and there are customers for the less expensive viands of Great Food Market, as there are customers for the Ajax Cut Price Supermarket. Price is no more an absolute as a marketing strategy than are other appeals. It is price *with* other factors and circumstances that makes a difference . . . that makes it the *right* price. It is right only in conjunction with your business goals, the surrounding circumstances, the effect they have on the customer's perception of reality and value. Here is what one young entrepreneur, a freelance writer, reported:

> Ten years ago, I was billing $30 an hour for copywriting.
> I kept losing bids and couldn't figure out why. Then I
> happened to talk with an acquaintance who'd just gone

out on her own after working at a large agency. She told me she was billing $60 an hour and had more work than she could handle. I was shocked: I had more experience and a better portfolio than she. I upped my rate to $45 overnight and started winning bids left and right. This experience taught me a great deal about perceived value and the role it plays in selecting a service provider. Obviously, a $60-an-hour writer was better than one who charged half of that, so she was the one who got hired.

What Is Price? What Is the *Right* Price?

Let us try to understand what price itself is: Price, it turns out, is not an absolute; it is a variable. Author and graduate school professor of business Jerry Rosenberg defines price in one of his many books, *Dictionary of Business Management* (John Wiley & Sons, Inc., 1993). It is, he reminds us, the money one actually receives for goods or services, not that amount of money for which one asks. His dictionary goes on to discuss and define 22 other terms using the word, such as *price stability, price rigidity, price control, price cutting*. Another book, *Business World 2*, by university professors Lawrence J. Gitman and Carl McDaniel, Jr. (Wiley, 1983), also has multiple discussions (28) of price and price-related terms, such as *price indexes, prestige pricing* and *objectives of pricing*. Price and pricing is thus obviously not a simple subject.

Price varies according to many factors and influences. One is the local market for similar services. Another is the hard facts of your costs, itself a critically important subject to which we shall shortly devote some time and attention. And still another is the set of individual circumstances and/or special considerations that may apply in a given situation, such as the client's demand for rush services, with a resulting need to charge premium rates for overtime, or a need to subcontract portions of a project to meet the customer's requirements.

These are contingencies that are likely to arise, not infrequently, and in developing your price structure you need to anticipate all such circumstances, rather than improvise on the spur of the moment. But then there are some arbitrary factors that reflect your strategic or policy decisions: For example, you may wish to do a given job as a loss leader or at breakeven to win a first job with a new client you expect to be an important one. You may prefer to establish inflexible fixed prices or you may prefer to negotiate prices for each job. You may prefer (or think the nature of your business requires) a sliding scale of prices, a roster of prices for carefully defined services or an hourly or daily rate. These may be arbitrary choices for you, in some cases, or they may be choices dictated by the nature of your business and perhaps customary practices in that business or industry. (It is sometimes much wiser to conform to established industry practice, rather than try to persuade customers to try to become adjusted to new and different ways of doing business.) Any of these factors may control your pricing policies, and so you may have more than one right price. In fact, the right price can vary widely, according to the philosophy or policy of the individual business owner. "Right" may refer to right in terms of a marketing consideration, rather than from an accounting or profit and loss viewpoint. The trade-offs may be 50 sales at a profit of $1 each versus 20 sales at a profit of $2 each. The 20 sales may be more profitable, in the end, because each sale may require 50 cents worth of shipping cost or 10 sales at a profit of $5 each. But there may also be the possibility of 15 sales at $4 gross profit each.

Obviously, there are many factors to consider. (Hence the great success and popularity of spreadsheet software, which helps you project the many variables to find the optimum solutions.)

Finally, the right price may be an arbitrary decision you make for whatever reason that motivates you. Some business owners are satisfied that the right price is one that recovers all their costs, including their own salary. The proprietor's salary or draw is not part of profit but is a *cost*, remember. It is chargeable to the business, as a regular cost, and ought to produce some profit for the business, just as would the salary of any other employee. You should thus draw enough salary to enable you to do the job properly and leave the client satisfied, but the business ought to make a profit on your labor. You and I launch our small enterprises with the general goal of becoming self-sufficient as independent practitioners or entrepreneurs of some sort. We plan to pay ourselves a decent salary, meet our bills, pay our taxes and stay out of trouble. Many of us do not consider the need to also take a bit of profit—net income beyond and above personal salary—to lay aside and pay for future growth and other nonroutine needs of the business and to sustain us during the valleys between the peaks of business and income. "Profit" is not a dirty word; it is the seed for future growth and a hedge against unforeseen and unexpected problems that beset us from time to time in business, as in our personal lives.

It helps greatly to think of "the business" as a separate entity—as your employer—that must earn a profit on your labor. One respondent on the CompuServe Consultant's forum recently remarked at how much his business improved when he had finally learned to think of what he was doing as a business, rather than as self-employment. He began to see himself as the employee of an entity he happened to own, although it was a sole proprietorship, that needed to earn a profit on his work.

Should you become incorporated, your corporation will, in fact and in law, be a separate entity legally and will automatically be your employer. It will withhold taxes, issue you a W2 form, provide whatever fringe benefits you should decide the corporation ought to pay for and otherwise function in all respects as an employer, even if you are the only employee of that corporation. In a practical sense, you are self-employed, perhaps, but in a legal sense, you are employed by the corporation. One not inconsiderable advantage of incorporating your business is that it helps you maintain that awareness of being an employee of a business entity, although there are other, more tangible benefits, such as a greater freedom to write off certain kinds of business expenses.

A Working Definition of the "Right" or Most Profitable Price

Considering the many variables suggested, there are many possible definitions of "the right price." But let's try to develop a working definition, excluding the special circumstances we have hypothesized here and setting aside the normal fears and inhibitions many of us have when we are still new to the competitive arena. Let us assume that you want to get the highest price you can for your service. That is a reasonable goal, one that is probably pursued by most sensible businesspeople.

On that basis, we might say that the right price is the highest one that fits your business strategy. Logically, it ought to be the highest price that you and your clients agree is justified by the value of the services you provide. And the major objective of this book is to help you get those highest prices by showing you how to be worth those top prices. That is an ideal, but there are exceptions, especially in the early phases of growing a business. You may very well be getting far less than you are worth, even after you have been maturing in business for a long time. That is not unusual, especially in one-person businesses, where the individual often has a strong tendency to greatly undervalue his or her services or to fear losing clients unless his or her prices are rock bottom.

The example of selling various quantities of something at various markups ought to make clear one of the difficulties of defining the "right" price. However, it also serves to illustrate the difficulty of defining the "top" price. Is "top" the highest price or the price that produces the greatest number of dollars in net profit? Did raising the markup bring in more dollars but cost you the future business of many customers? That is, did you lose more in the long term than you gained in the short term?

Those are questions that are not easy to answer, but they are questions you should ask yourself in deciding your pricing and marketing policies. They are questions that you need to ask yourself in deciding what your services are or should be worth to a customer.

Perhaps the problem is in that term "worth." What *are* you—your services, that is—worth? What do *you* think your services are worth? More to the point, what does *your client* think your services are worth? Would you be surprised that you probably underestimate that latter figure—that many of your clients value your services more highly than you think? That is often the case.

It is exceedingly difficult to see yourself as others see you, as the poet said.

One way of finding out what customers perceive as the right price is by testing. This is quite a common practice—even one considered to be mandatory in mail order. In principle, it's quite easy to do: You make test mailings. You might, for example, test your price by mailing three mailings at three different prices and then evaluate how addressees react. You find out how many orders you can get at each price, and you then evaluate the results of each test to see what price is in your best interest. It may or may not be the highest price, for reasons already explained.

Testing is fairly easy to do in mail order but much more difficult to do in other modes of marketing. In mail order, you can select mailing lists of equal size that resemble each other quite closely, so that the results ought to be a fair sample of the entire list to which you wish to send your offer. That microcosm of your whole market is much more difficult to isolate for test purposes in other, less controllable modes of marketing except, perhaps, for telemarketing. There it ought to be easily possible to try several different prices with equivalent classes of prospects.

That does not mean you must be trying to get the highest price. In all fairness, we must recognize that not every seller tries to get the highest price possible. Not trying to get the top price may be the result of underestimating the worth of what one does for customers and even of underestimating what customers would be willing to pay for what you do for them. But that is not necessarily the case: Many highly successful businesses have been built on the basis of offering the lowest possible prices as a major business strategy. As a rule, these are businesses dealing in physical products—usually such consumer goods as clothing, appliances, carpets and automobiles.

Service businesses are usually much more difficult to base on discount principles (except as loss leaders) because it is most difficult, in most cases, to sell services at bargain rates and survive, much less turn real profits. If you wished to discount your services, just what is it that you would discount or how would you demonstrate that what you were offering was truly a discount? There really is not such a thing as a list price for a service, although there are apparent market prices. For example, most repair services—TV, plumbing, dishwasher and electrical—are based on some service charge for the original call, and in some highly competitive repair businesses, such as TV repair, there are many apparent bargains. That idea can be applied to other service businesses when there is some recognizable unit that represents the service or the chief objective of the service to a prospect. Thus, some resume writers may offer something on the order of "Resumes from $7.50 up" as a special attraction. Still, the term "discount" is not truly appropriate here and is not often used as an appeal in selling services. When a service provider wants to offer the appeal of low price, the more typical approach is to offer a "special" of one kind or another as a leader or lure. Here, the right price may be whatever "special" price attracts the greatest number of customers and still leaves the way open to turn a profit on the work. That $7.50 resume may be for some absolute minimum service, such as editing and word-processing one's one-page resume, written in draft by the customer. That leaves ample room to sell the customer a much-expanded service or additional services so that the $7.50 resume is rarely, if ever, a reality.

Let us look at the question of the right price yet another way. The definition of the right price, for your purposes, may change over the course of developing your business. The right price for you when you are getting your business established may not be the same right price you plan to get eventually, when your business has become well established with a regular clientele. A different set of circumstances may mandate a different pricing policy as your business matures. As in many other things in business, be alert for changes and ready to adapt everything, even pricing policy, to the dictates of new and changed circumstances.

The definitions proposed or possible include valuable provisions by implication: They imply that your services can vary in their value to the client. The price you can command for them, the price a client is willing to pay, that is, also varies according to the current market value of the services. But to at least some extent the kind of service you provide and its value is under your control.

You can provide service of a value that justifies and enables you to get the high price you wish to get for your service. Value is not, or ought not to be, a chance occurrence; it is, or ought to be, a carefully designed element but highly variable in more than one respect. Here is an example of one set of variables that has such an effect of offering more than one value, justifying a scale of prices:

I recently had to have repair service for one of my computer monitors. The service establishment I called—I selected the firm from among a number of advertisers in the Yellow Pages—offered me a range of rates for a variety of services they offered. The options offered included pickup and delivery service versus my own carry-in of the monitor to their shop, and priority of service—while-you-wait, 24-hour and 24-hour to two-week service, the latter variable depending on how busy the shop is at the time. That left it up to me to determine what I needed and what I was willing to pay for.

That is one way to correlate prices with value, to bring the client into the picture and get the client's agreement that the price you are asking is the right one for the service the client wants. The value is a variable, and the customer helps decide what the value is and what it is worth. That is one way to solve the dilemma of pricing—by offering several options of service—and the idea is adaptable to a great many enterprises. However, it is not a model that fits all cases. There are others that we shall discuss.

Price and the Measure of Success

Price bears some relationship to success, but the definition of success is elusive, at least partly because it does not mean the same thing to everyone. For that matter, success is a goal, often never achieved because many of us (probably most of us) keep raising the goal. Perhaps success is viewed initially as earning $25,000 a year, but when you reach that, you may elevate it to $50,000 a year. Success may be a snug, three-bedroom cottage—until you have it. Then you dream of a five-bedroom country home. But let's try to define success as a possible first goal for the new entrepreneur:

Among the factors that are generally accepted by observers as signs of a successful business are the ability to

1. pay your bills, your taxes and your own salary, with a profit to provide for the inevitable contingencies;

2. keep your customers satisfied and therefore coming back with repeat business, while recommending you to others; and

3. grow—not necessarily in size because that is often merely swelling, rather than growing—but in overall capability and in stability of your business base.

If you manage to do all these things, you may count yourself at least a success in business, successful enough to survive those critical first years. (Venture capitalists tend to regard breakeven operation reached by the end of the third or fourth year a reasonable goal.)

Success is not an absolute. There are degrees of success—at least by popular opinion. Some businesses are deemed to be more successful than others. The degree of success is inferred by observers of what they deem to be evidence: The size of the business, its growth rate and its external appearance—expensive offices or showrooms, flashy advertising and other physical manifestations of what the business can afford. From these signs, observers infer profitability and magnitude of success.

Especially, the inference is that high prices mean great profits. Of course, customers also expect to encounter higher prices here than in doing business with firms exhibiting a more modest "front." Many people, therefore, reverse the cause and effect: Rather than think success leads to the establishment of an impressive front, they conclude that creating an impressive front leads to success! More specifically, they think that the front enables them to set and get the right price—i.e., the highest possible price—and that, they believe, leads directly to such high profitability and business success.

Are these impressions accurate? Is the business with all the symbols of great success actually more successful—more profitable—than others with much less "flash" or, apparently, less "class"? Does getting the highest prices automatically ensure high profits and great success?

These are among the matters yet to be explored here, and the answers may surprise and disillusion you, but it is important to know them and avoid self-deceit. Few things are more deadly in their results than to indulge yourself in pet notions that have no real basis in fact, and we shall look at some of these.

Success versus Survival

A disheartening number of small businesses fail to meet all the objectives listed earlier as minimal standards to achieve the modest goal of minimal business success, including operating at a profit and thus accumulating a fund for future needs.

Success means or should mean that you are able to draw from your business an adequate salary, one that is commensurate with your labor and skills. Bear that in mind when interpreting everything you read in these pages. You ought to be *building* a successful business, and that may take some time. However, you must not let subsidizing your own business, by drawing inadequate compensation from it, become a permanent means of sustaining that business. A subsidy may be necessary at first, and if it is, treat that labor as "sweat equity," part of your investment in your business. But if it is necessary to do that or otherwise keep your business alive at your personal expense, be sure that that is temporary. Do it only while you are establishing a foundation and building a business. Never lose sight of the fact that you must expect your business to support you eventually, and not the reverse.

Completely aside from that special circumstance where we may feel compelled to make personal sacrifices and undercut the market initially to get started, many of us charge too little for our services even under normal circumstances when it is no longer necessary. Often, we do so in ignorance, not realizing that we are charging prices that allow us little or no profit at all. The fact that we are managing to pay our bills, our taxes and our own modest salary leads us into an illusion of success. But we also do so, far too often, in fear of being unable to close sales unless we are more competitive than our competitors are, where "competitive" means cheaper. Thus, it is possible that we may justifiably deem the lowest price possible to be the right price for that time and circumstance, but it should be right only for that time and circumstance, not as a general principle of operations. It is not necessary, nor even desirable, to close every possible sale. There are often sales we ought not to close and customers with whom we ought not to do business.

This latter situation is probably the most typical one for small, usually one- or two-person businesses, often home-based. Those circumstances are deceptive to the inexperienced businessperson, who is thus deluded as to the real cost of doing business. Such businesspeople often assume that their business operates at almost no cost and thus that income is almost all gross profit. For this reason, among the first and most important matters is education in the cost of doing business. That brings us to the subject of accounting, the function of every business venture that tells us what our minimum prices ought to be.

One of the near-tragedies of small business is that the failure to meet all normal business objectives does not mean you will be forced to abandon your business. That truth is both good news and bad news. It's good news insofar as it is a way for the individual to survive a difficult period, where the larger company might well go under. The bad news is that some individuals come to regard this as a permanent state of affairs. The unfortunate truth is that a great many practitioners compromise with true success and accept a substitute: They continue in practice by settling for an inadequate personal income. They subsidize their own ventures by drawing a much smaller salary than they ought to, by not charging their businesses for out-of-pocket expenses they incur and by otherwise making sacrifices to stay in business.

That is not a mistake only if and when it is used as a means for getting started in building a business or perhaps breaking into an unusually competitive market so that you can later profit properly from the business. It is not a mistake if it is done knowingly and deliberately for such purposes. In that case, it is an investment in marketing, helping to establish sales and clientele. Many highly successful businesses have resulted from such beginnings. In that phase of growing a business from nothing—lifting yourself by your bootstraps—the right price may be one that is low enough to attract a few initial customers.

The mistake lies in permitting such price cutting to become a permanent mode of operation; then, it represents failure, not success. It brings to mind a well-known cartoon in which a seedy individual is scrounging cigarettes from the gutter, with the caption, "Yeah, I used to be the low bidder."

On the other hand, in business one develops sales strategies, and there are cases where you may be able to *appear* to be the low bidder, even when you are not, in fact, the lowest bidder. Or, better yet, you may be able to show that in a real sense you are the low bidder because you offer so much value per dollar of cost than competitors do.

The Meaning of Value

Value is a word that marketers tend to use rather loosely. Advertising and sales literature is full of hyperbolic claims of value, often with adjectives such as "great" and "unrivaled" that are intended to dramatize and stress the claim. Still, value is not a frivolous subject but a quite serious one, one that has a great deal to do with your ability to command good rates for your services. The subject deserves more than a paragraph or two or even a page or two. Let us get on to an extended discussion of the subject in the next chapter where we can explore it together.

Chapter 2

Adding Value To Support Your Price

Value is a variable and salable asset. Marketers like to speak of value as though it were an absolute and fixed quality, but it is not. It is, or can be, a manageable asset for the resourceful entrepreneur and has, or can be made to have, a great influence on how customers perceive the worth of your services.

The Meaning of Value

My online dictionary (*American Heritage* edition) defines nine different kinds of value, and there are still other kinds that this dictionary does not mention. The many kinds of value are defined by qualifying the word with an adjective, as in *prestige* value, *intrinsic* value, *market* value and *perceived* value. On the other hand, we also encounter *added* value as a business concept, and the use of value as an adjective, as in *value management, value engineering* and *value analysis,* three terms for what is essentially the same thing: A method for enhancing value through an organized discipline that is aimed at cutting costs without reducing quality or effectiveness. (More on this shortly.)

There is also what is known as a "VAR" or Value Added Retailer. That refers to a retailer who does something to items he or she buys at wholesale and thus improves or modifies the items in some way that increases their value or market price. This is recognized in many states by imposing a "VAT"—Value Added Tax—on VARs.

These few examples demonstrate that value is not an absolute or sharply defined quality or asset but is actually a complex and multifaceted idea. One could even argue that value exists only in the mind as a human perception and has no existence outside of that perception. That view of value as a human perception is most useful in making value a business reality, an asset that can be controlled and managed, as the term *value management* clearly suggests. Most important, however, is that value management can be a most important business asset, once you have a good understanding of it in all its manifestations and potential uses—and, especially, in how it can influence prices and sales. Having that knowledge of and appreciation for value will help you greatly to maximize the prices you will be able to command—that is, the rates your customers will willingly pay you for what you do. You will begin to understand, for example, why there are many computer programmers who struggle to find contracts at $40 per hour while others have all the work they can handle at $75 and more per hour.

A short time ago you met the term VAR here, an acronym for value added retailer, which refers to anyone who processes items to increase their value and sells the improved items at retail. The EC/EDI (Electronic Commerce/Electronic Data Interchange) is a highly sophisticated system I first learned of via the Internet. It is a system still in development under government subsidies. Its purpose overall is to accelerate and make more efficient a great deal of commerce by processing the documents—quotations, bids, contracts, reports and, in some cases, even the products—via electronic networks and related communications. Its literature includes this definition of a VAN, Value Added Network, an important element in the system: *A company that provides communications services, electronic mailboxing and other communications services for EDI transmissions.* The VAN thus increases the value of the communications system by adding such services as mailboxes and other items that facilitate the transactions for which the system is designed. It is another example of enhancing and increasing the value of an end product by some process of adding to the original value, improving that cost-to-results ratio. This idea can be applied to any business under the philosophy that there is always a better way to do something—a more efficient and less costly way, that is.

In the more familiar setting of conventional business relationships, adding value may involve tangible, physical products, as well as, or in place of, adding or enhancing services. For example, a retailer might buy "plain vanilla" computers and add components and popular software programs to them before reselling them. I recently bought such a computer system. Two very large computer retailers, with their huge stores directly across the street from each other, offered systems that were just about what I was seeking, and the two had almost identical prices. One, however, had a great deal more software already installed in the system and included in the price. The practice of adding value to a computer by preinstalling software in it is a not uncommon practice today in the computer industry. And in that industry there are also many small businesses based on buying standard components and assembling them into operating computers. The labor and skills of assembling the components and testing the final product represent value added to the components, entitling the assembler to a profit.

Something akin to that exists as the organized discipline referred to earlier and known as *value analysis* or *value management*, although it originated as *value engineering* and still exists as an engineering discipline. In fact, there is an association of engineers named SAVE, Society of American Value Engineers, who practice value engineering. Briefly, value engineering is an organized method for studying a product, system, process or other item to determine how costs can be reduced and/or efficiency and utility increased without sacrificing quality or usefulness. In brief, although its primary goal is reducing costs, it is a discipline that has as its objective the improving of the cost-to-results ratio in other ways. That may involve making parts of less expensive but equally effective materials or eliminating parts that do not add materially to the usefulness of the item but only increase its cost. Many relevant aspects of the methods are transferable generally to increasing the value of the services you offer and thus the rates you are entitled to charge and ought to command. But let us first go on to examine just what some of these various kinds of value are and why the term, "value," is used in so many different contexts to mean so many different things.

A Few Kinds of Value

Probably the value most of us think of is intrinsic value. A gold ring may contain $60 worth of gold, and $60 would be its *intrinsic* value. However, *esteem* value has been added to the gold by fashioning it into an item of jewelry, so it now has greater value than an equivalent lump of gold. It may be worth several hundred dollars in the marketplace as a result. That would be its *market* value. However, suppose it is an antique. That could add to its value—to its market value. And suppose it was once owned by an important historical figure, such as King George III or George Washington. That would increase its market value further, perhaps to many thousands of dollars. At least, collectors of such objects might perceive its value to be many thousands of dollars, although you and I might not. Or it might be the work of an especially accomplished artisan whose name and reputation are well known and highly regarded. That could add greatly to its esteem value, which is, of course, a *perceived* value. It is a variable, as you can easily gather when you attend an auction sale and witness bidders dropping out as the cost goes beyond and above the limits they have put on the value of the object of the bidding. If the bidders are dealers intending to resell the objects, the bids they submit reflect their estimates of the market values of the objects. If they are collectors, their bids reflect the esteem values they personally assign the objects. So the bidder dropping out may be a dealer who has an idea of how much he or she could resell the item for and drops out when the price has gone to a point where that bidder sees no profit in buying the item. Still, the principle of perceived value applies here: The dealer has set a *resale* value on the object, based on a perception of what the item would bring in a resale— i.e., what the dealer's customers would perceive as its value.

All of this makes it clear that value is a most flexible quality. If you attend a few auction sales, you should soon perceive that auctioneers are salesmen and saleswomen, and the best ones are quite skilled in persuading bidders of the great value represented by each item offered up for bids. Auctioneers are, as all skilled sales specialists are, themselves value managers of a quite special kind!

The Management of Value

That illustrates the many facets of value, and it introduces the subject of control or management of value through shaping or management of perceptions. Perhaps value is always only a perception, and a fixed value, such as the market value of an item, is a perception that many hold in common. It can be almost impossible to determine the market value of such an item as the ring discussed above because it is a unique item, and the value of a unique object is whatever buyers are willing to pay to own it. Rare objects, such as that ring, statuary, paintings and other such items are therefore often sold at auction. That is probably the most practical way to determine what their value is: No one has yet found a more efficient or more effective way to determine what value buyers will place on such objects. At a public auction, interested people will establish values by whatever amounts they are willing to offer for the items. So perceived value can vary according to the preconceived notions or opinions of those who do the perceiving. Note too that, to a large degree, the values are set by observing what others are willing to pay: Most of us have a strong tendency to be influenced by what others think. If a great many people offer hundreds of dollars for some object that we thought to be worth far less, we may very well spontaneously upgrade our own perception of the worth of that object.

Many localities have regularly scheduled auction sales where a wide variety of merchandise is sold. Some of the merchandise is distressed (has minor flaws), some is surplus and is being sacrificed to get rid of it, and some is priced at everyday prices and does not represent a bargain of any kind. Public auction has that advantage of lending itself to the management of perceptions of value.

Actually, I touched on that idea obliquely in Chapter 1 in discussing the use of testing prices to determine which price produced the best results. Akin to the principle of the auction sale, testing is a method for asking prospective buyers what they think something is worth. It's a sound idea because value is a perception. In practice, the lowest price does not always produce the largest number of orders. One man ran a tiny classified advertisement to sell a small item for $2 and did quite well with it. He decided that he could greatly expand his sales by offering the item for $1. To his dismay, sales dropped off sharply at $1. The public decided the item couldn't be very good if he wanted only $1 for it. The manufacturer of a new hair spray had a similar experience in offering a product for $1.98 when no competitive product was offered at under $2.98. The item languished in the stores until the manufacturer raised the price to $2.98. Customers refused to have faith in a hair spray that was so much cheaper than they were accustomed to paying for such a product.

Perception is also responsible for esteem value, mentioned earlier, the pride one takes in acquiring and owning some item. In general, this perception of value is of two general kinds. You may have already noted that many people like to report, most triumphantly, how they cleverly negotiated a great bargain for some item. They take great pride in being good shoppers or great negotiators, and so they report with great glee how cheaply they bought something or other. On the other hand, there are those who take the opposite tack and are most proud of how expensive some possession of theirs is—what a princely sum they spent to acquire it. One couple won a large TV set as a prize and were happily congratulating themselves on winning what they were sure was worth at least $500. They lost their enthusiasm and were quite disappointed to learn that the set could be bought for less than $400. Remember the bromide that "you get what you pay for"? That is a creed a great many people use to justify regarding a bargain with great suspicion and placing faith in high prices as guarantors of high quality.

Door-to-door sellers of merchandise learn that it helps their sales effectiveness to report to a prospect which of his or her neighbors have been customers. "Oh, yes, I sold one of these fine vacuum cleaners to your neighbor, Mrs. Daugherty, at 4211 just last week," seems to inspire more trust in the seller and the value of the seller's products. It also tends to arouse the message in the prospect's mind, "Well, if she can afford it, I can too," which helps greatly in winning the sale. Keeping up with the Joneses is also an influence that shapes many people's perceptions of value.

Walter A. Sheaffer, who later became well known for his Sheaffer fountain pens, products of high quality, originally sold organs. He had tried for all of a long afternoon to sell one to Farmer Hockersmith, but to no avail. Hockersmith enjoyed the free private concert but did not buy. But Sheaffer was determined to make this sale. The next day he loaded his most expensive organ into the wagon and drove out into the country, past the Hockersmith place on the road that led to Farmer Hartwick's place. As he started to pass the Hockersmith's house, Tillie Hockersmith called out to him to ask if he was headed up to the Hartwicks.

Sheaffer just nodded hello and asked, "Who else around here could afford the best organ available?"

The Hockersmiths went to work immediately to "induce" Sheaffer to sell them the fine organ he appeared to be delivering to the Hartwicks.

There are many ways to influence others' notions or impressions and thus manage even perceived value to at least some extent. We have shown this for special cases, such as jewelry, objects of art or historical objects, but it applies also to more ordinary products and their values, for the principles are exactly the same. But perhaps our methods do not always influence and shape perceptions as much as they screen and sort customers into classes, such as those who are more comfortable with paying high prices and those who take pride in finding or negotiating bargains. However, the end result is the same, whether we truly understand the trigger mechanism or not.

When I was a schoolboy working in a drugstore after school, I was struck by the difference between two brands of rubbing alcohol we sold. Mifflin was the name brand and sold for 17 cents in a rather fancy, hourglass-shaped pint bottle, bearing a distinctive label. We sold another brand, an unfamous one, in the plainest of pint bottles, with the plainest of labels, for 8 cents a bottle. The contents were the same, despite the great difference in price. I later worked, as an adult, in a field that included industrial products and was thus able to verify the idea that perceived value can influence price.

As I proceeded to gain experience in the world of business and commerce, I saw more and more examples of how meaningless and yet meaningful brand names are: Meaningless in terms of significant differences between and among the many brands of a given product, but meaningful in terms of what brand names can mean as business assets that contribute to black ink on the ledgers. I saw how distillers sell each other whisky in barrels, so that the bottle you buy with a Seagram label may contain the product of a Hiram Walker distillery. I went to a Sylvania distributor to buy parts for an RCA portable TV that was manufactured by Sylvania and retailed with both Sylvania and RCA labels. (The parts cost less at the Sylvania parts distributor.) I learned that Bayer and other brand aspirins are chemically identical, but a great many people (including my own wife) put their trust in the more expensive brands with the widely advertised and better-known names.

That behavior is probably more common than ever today, with the enormous abundance of consumer goods available. Name brands are always much more expensive than lesser-known brands. Perhaps the name-brand soup is a better-tasting soup than the store-brand soup in some cases, but in many cases the two products are identical and are made on the same assembly line. The differences between alternative brands (i.e., the alternative packages and their labels) are quite often only the differences that exist in the buyer's mind. It is not uncommon for the name brands to have much more expensive packaging than the "store" or "private" brands, however. In many cases, such as perfumes and cosmetics generally, the package may be more costly than the contents. It is fair to say that in such cases (and in many others) the dealer is selling the package not the contents. In fact, that is more general a truth than you might imagine, as you will see shortly when we get to a discussion of what it is that a business—every business—really sells, a discussion that may offer a surprise or two as recognition of certain facts forms.

There are many other examples of perceived values and their relevant influences, closely akin to some of the earlier examples, but with this difference: With some products, such as jewelry, art, perfume and clothing, prestige alone, as perceived by the customer (and carefully nurtured by the marketer) is a great factor affecting the buyer's decision. With many other kinds of products, the customer is persuaded by advertising and promotion to distinguish between an original and a copy or knockoff or between the "genuine" article and an "imitation." That is why so much advertising stresses claims of being "genuine," "original" or "the real thing," while urging the reader to beware of being misled by imitations. The implication is, clearly, that the "genuine" brand is of much greater value than any other brand. Sometimes we refer to "designer brands," where it is the name and reputation of the designer that is sold to the customer. It is that same strategic principle that underlies decisions to create and register trademarks, trade names and logos, and otherwise publicize and protect all devices that somehow distinguish a company and its products. Once established, such symbols of distinction can add great value to the company and its products to prove that the products are "genuine."

There was, for example, a time when the fountain pen considered by many to be the very best was a green one with a distinguishing white dot, manufactured by the W.A. Sheaffer Co. Not only was this fountain pen believed to be the best one; it was a symbol of distinction to own one of these, and those who owned them displayed them proudly. (In high school, I personally envied those students who were fortunate enough to own one of these famous fountain pens.)

The distinctive symbols known as trademarks, service marks and logos (an abbreviation of logotype) become important assets to their owners, who guard them legally by registering them. Among the most familiar ones are those of IBM, RCA, GE, Hertz, Avis, American Airlines, Armour and Toyota, and they become known in the farthest reaches of the world through their advertising. Frequently the trademark or logo is more familiar to the casual observer than is the name of the organization (would "International Business Machines" ring a bell with you as quickly as "IBM" does?), but it represents a specific kind of name recognition and delivers the usual benefits of that recognition. And sometimes a title, trademark or logo is such that a strange thing happens: When reading or hearing the name for the first time, many individuals have a sense of deja vu that deceives them into believing that they recognize the name as a familiar and long-established one. That is a somewhat strange phenomenon, but human nature being what it is, such a thing does happen, as the following example will demonstrate.

"Great Northern TV Service" was one such name. It was the trade name of a small (one-person) business in Philadelphia that had not been in existence a long time. However, the name proved to be an impressive and memorable one to many people, so that a surprisingly large number of customers somehow deceived themselves into believing that they had long known the name and recognized it as a familiar one belonging to a large company. It was thus an odd case of name recognition, for the recognition was imaginary and so spurious, but it had the same effect that genuine name recognition would have had. The very name of the business *seemed* right, perhaps because it rolled off the tongue so easily and gracefully, and it inspired confidence in customers. The entrepreneur who traded under that name was trying only to establish an image of dependability. (Compare "Great Northern TV Service" with "Sam's TV Service" to understand his objective.) He succeeded, to his surprise, to a much greater degree than he had planned or anticipated. (Once again, we can see the magic resulting from the guidance and influencing of human perception, even if unintentional. And we can see, also, how little we understand or can predict outcomes, unless we test or somehow otherwise pursue and gain an objective view.)

One point to be made here is that the choice of name can be important, but making the right choice is more art than science. The objective is to find a name that is not merely ostentatious or imposing but is somehow fitting for the enterprise. Many budding entrepreneurs opt for a long and, presumably, overwhelmingly impressive name, such as World Wide Information & Technology Sciences Corporation. These too often prove to be ponderous and awkward, and thus they become self-defeating. Some will force-fit words into a name of which the initial letters form an acronym. And there are those entrepreneurs who make the mistake of working overtime to be clever and subtle and come up with a name that does not begin to define to the public at large what the business offers prospective customers. For example, one entrepreneur launched his computer consulting service with the name "Ones and Zeros," a name that was attention-getting but was also thoroughly mystifying to all those who are completely unaware of the binary arithmetic system upon which computer technology is based. Even those who are expert in computers might not make the connection, so the cleverness of the name is wasted there too.

Image Is Itself a Benefit

The main point is that image counts, in many ways, but especially in what it does for the perceived value of your services. Customers pay for image, as well as for other benefits. (Yes, image—the confidence and comfort the right image confers on the client—is a benefit customers enjoy and you can therefore sell.) Here, as in so many other aspects of successful business practice, you must be able to somehow perceive yourself—your enterprise—through the customer's eyes.

The psychology of image works with me, too, as much as it does with those who are completely unaware or unthinking of marketing principles: I pay dealer prices, well aware that they are high when compared with many competitive automobile repair shops, to have my automobile serviced. I pay for the immaculately clean service floor, the technician dressed in a clean uniform, the protective cloth draped over my seat before the technician gets behind the wheel of my car, the old parts deposited in my car in a clean box or bag, the comfortable waiting room, the apparent professionalism of all the personnel with whom I deal and all the other evidences of a well-organized and well-run operation. That includes—especially—the comfort I get from seeing the manufacturer's plainly marked factory-training vehicle parked behind the service department, lending credence to the dealer's claims of "factory-trained technicians." It all puts my mind at ease, with the feeling that I am in good hands when I bring my car in to the dealer's premises for service. That "in good hands" perception is a decided business asset, one that you can sell to a public that wants such assurance. (Witness the large insurance company for whom that image of cupped, welcoming and sheltering hands is a logo of long standing.)

The Image You Will Have

You—your business, that is—will acquire an image, as time goes by, whether you set out to do so deliberately or not. Even if you make no conscious effort to create that image or to control and shape it, your customers will decide for themselves who and what you are. If you leave it to chance, your customers will decide for themselves whether you are the cheapest guy in town, someone who charges too much for what you do, a "quick and dirty" service, a highly professional service, someone who takes advantage of customers, someone who treats customers fairly, or as any of many other possible characterizations. On the other hand, you can decide what you wish the public—your customers and prospective customers—to see, and you can then take steps to project that image so that there can be no doubt about it. That is a decision you can and should make for yourself as a deliberate choice. It will have a great deal to do with the kind of success you enjoy.

You don't—really can't—make a decision about the image you wish to build without considering a few other things. You will first have to make decisions up front about your business goals in general and about the kind of clientele you wish to attract.

In every trade or business, there are those who are or get the reputations (image, that is) for being the cheapest guys in town, the most upscale and most expensive, or one of those who are scattered along the spectrum between those two extremes. Which reputation do you want to get? More to the point, what kind of trade (read "what kind of customers" or "what kind of market") are you pursuing or did you decide you wanted when you planned your business? Whichever segment you pursue, the high end, low end or middle, you will get some of all segments, but you will depend mainly on the segment you decided to pursue, consciously or unconsciously. (Yes, a great many entrepreneurs do not deliberately plan the market segments they will pursue, but they still make that decision unconsciously by the way they go about their marketing and image building.)

You will gradually acquire an image, complete with several outstanding characteristics that may or may not be accurate, but they will be what your customers see, unless you take measures to control what they see. They may come to see you as someone who is meticulous or someone who is rather casual about details, as someone who always delivers as promised or someone who always needs to be pressed to get the job done, as someone who always delivers the very highest quality, or as someone who always delivers only "get by" quality, etc.

Here is a brief dialogue between a young computer programmer who was explaining her dilemma to an older, more experienced computer consultant. It happens to illustrate the point here quite well:

QUESTION: My prospective client is offering a fixed-price contract that is well below my quoted price, which was based on my hourly rate and estimated hours to complete the job. This client will probably not pay more than he offered. Should I walk away with my fixed, nonnegotiable rates and lose a prospective client, or should I sell my services for less than they are worth?

RESPONSE: Mary, never sell your services for less than they are worth. Maybe your prospective client needs to be educated about why you're worth the price you quoted. Negotiating is a two-way street, but you will lose credibility with this client if you cut your rates without negotiating a corresponding reduction in the requirement or in what you guarantee to deliver. You can negotiate the deadline, services offered and your guarantee, for example, but do negotiate; never just cut your price arbitrarily.

Here are a couple more reports along the same line, these from freelance writers:

When I first started working on my own I thought I'll set my rates low, about $45 an hour. I lost a lot of bids to higher priced consultants and could not understand why at first. Eventually I realized that the customers thought I wasn't as experienced as my higher priced competitors. When I doubled my rates, I immediately started closing more deals. It has to do with perceived value.

While I was in college I started doing resumes for people at $45 a pop. I had an easier time getting business when my rate went to $125 to $200.

Obviously, these are not isolated cases but are indicative of the general case. A great many people judge quality or worth by price alone, especially when they have little else in the way of standards by which to judge.

Choosing Your Customers

A point many of us tend to miss in launching a business is that we can get the kind of patronage we want, if we plan properly for it and execute the plan faithfully. What you can't get, normally, is a complete collection of all kinds. That is, you can decide you want an upscale and select clientele and organize your business accordingly to appeal to and attract that kind of clientele. That would normally mean you would have a limited number of customers at high rates. You can decide, however, that you want to do a high-volume business: Many customers. You might very well then judge that you will have to be greatly competitive—read "low-priced"—to succeed in that approach. It is difficult, almost impossible, to do both because you cannot be both kinds of supplier. (Yes, the exclusive department stores often have it both ways by having "bargain basements," but that is a special case and not applicable here at all.) Generally speaking, most of us must decide to have it one way or the other. But it requires more than an arbitrary decision. It requires understanding of customer psychology, for one, and it requires setting things up to project the image you need to capture the market segment you want.

One simple example is that of the storefront lawyer versus the law firm in a high-rise office building with deep carpets, costly furnishings and a "good address." The large corporate client is not likely to patronize the storefront lawyer, just as the citizen involved in an automobile accident or similar claim is not likely to attempt to enlist the services of that law firm in a large suite of offices on the 18th floor at one of the best addresses in the city.

Newspaper and Yellow Pages advertising offers many familiar examples. At the moment, one of the "hot" fields is the Internet, that highly publicized "information superhighway." A large number of access providers—those who provide the connection between your own computer and the Internet via your telephone line—are advertising frantically, offering rates as low as $9.95 per month. They thus assure themselves of a clientele seeking the cheapest guys in town. But that doesn't deter other suppliers who charge more. One, who does not advertise in the newspapers and offers service at $23 per month as the lowest price for only the most basic service, a "shell account" ($35 per month for a fuller set of services), is prospering. His success is easily understandable: He provides services that make access to the Internet easy for the least skilled, least experienced user, and he is highly responsive to his subscribers with easy-to-use facilities and an obvious eagerness to please. To a great many people, that is worth more than a bargain price.

Another access provider pursues an entirely different course, one that requires a special explanation. Whereas most of the access providers are trying to build as large a subscription list as possible, this supplier pursues a middle course. He provides what constitutes a full service for $20 per month, but he is not basing the success of his business on the number of subscribers he can enroll. Quite the contrary, he bases his success on the ancillary services he offers subscribers, such as renting space for "home pages" and general consulting services relevant to the Internet and, especially, establishing and maintaining a presence on the Internet. He knows exactly the kind of customers he wants: His goal is to find and sign up the kind of subscriber who is most likely to want those ancillary services. His personal interest is to provide maximum net income, of course, but his business philosophy is considerably more refined than the simple one of trying to scoop up the maximum number of subscribers.

That "target marketing" constitutes a special kind of business strategy. It entails setting rates to attract a certain, well-defined class of clientele to whom more profitable services may be sold. That does not mean setting rates at the lowest or the highest possible level; it means setting them at whatever level will attract the kind of customers who are good prospects for those other services that you really want to sell. Winning new customers is expensive, and many businesses lose money on every first sale to a new customer—catalog houses, for example—but the objective is to win new customers to whom many more sales can be made.

Of course, the difference is not merely in the setting of the rate structure but also in the entire marketing strategy and methodology—in where and how you advertise and in your marketing strategies and methods generally. It is a matter of whether your goal (and strategy) is to make sales or to make customers.

Many businesses and professions—most, in fact—depend on this kind of two-step marketing process. For the dentist, for example, the making of dentures is far more profitable than the filling of teeth. In my own case, when I published a newsletter, the real rewards were in the consulting projects that resulted from the circulation of that publication; the annual subscription fees could never of themselves have constituted an ample income. In fact, many businesses publish newsletters that do not turn a profit and may even be operated at a loss, but the newsletters are run as marketing tools, which justifies subsidies.

It thus becomes clear that in such cases as these, the "right price" is the one that will attract the desired clientele in the greatest numbers possible. One hundred of the right customers may thus be far more profitable than 500 of another class of customers.

What Do You Really Sell?

Probably the most important question concerning value—the value of whatever you sell, that is—is what it represents to your customers. Just what *is* it that you sell? In fact, and more importantly, never mind what you sell: What is it that your customers buy?

You may understand this better if you adopt the view expressed by many in advertising that everyone is in a service business, no matter what they sell or think they are selling. That concept points out that customers do not buy things; they buy what things do.

As one marketing expert put it, people don't buy quarter-inch drills; they buy quarter-inch holes. That begins to approach the essence of marketing, but there are even more subtle factors at work in a great many cases. For one, there is the emotional element, usually a much more persuasive influence than reason.

The late Elmer Wheeler, who was popularly known as "America's greatest salesman," had an unusual understanding of this, and he had a great knack for perceiving and expressing this idea. Probably his best known admonition to all marketers was, for example, "Sell the sizzle, not the steak." He is also credited with saying, "If you want to sell them lemonade, you have to first make

them thirsty." In one case, challenged by a retailer to help get rid
of a large overstock of long underwear, Wheeler managed the task
successfully by making a huge display of the merchandise with a
prominent sign that said, "THEY DON'T ITCH." It proved to be
a much more powerful appeal than the word "SALE."

These aphorisms invoke the well-known principle, pointed
out to everyone who has made an effort to learn the principles of
sales and advertising, of selling benefits, not features. Unfortunately, not everyone understands the difference. Let us take the
simple example of that resume-writing service again.

Among those things that one may regard as benefits are choices
of typefaces, number of printed copies, availability of a great as-
sortment of formats, offering of costly papers, great resume-
writing experience and other such boons to job seekers. In the
context we are using here, those are features, not benefits. They
may be used to explain *how* your resumes achieve great benefits
for your customers, but they are not the benefits per se. The benefits per se are what your resumes *do* for your customers—help
them in finding a job or help in finding a better job. Or, better yet,
they help find a way to win a more satisfying and happier existence
or a way to escape an unhappy existence in a hated job. These
kinds of promises are what customers want to hear and will influence their decision making and their assessing the value of your
services. Yes, your customers do know that a better resume increases their chances for that job or better job to which they
aspire, but the appeal is in presenting them the promise of winning
that desired benefit—not the job, but what the job represents to
them.

Analysis To Find the Real Benefit

That pundit who observed that people who buy quarter-inch drills
are really out to buy quarter-inch holes was on the right track to
understanding customer motivation but still had at least one step
further to take in his analysis: Quarter-inch holes are not a benefit.
People want quarter-inch holes because they need them in their

work or they want to do "handyman" kinds of things. The benefit may be any of several things—pride or satisfaction of owning the best quarter-inch drill, the ability to be the "handiest" kind of person around the house, or being admired by fellow workers as the owner of the best tool of its kind. All of these are possible benefits, emotional benefits, for the most part. To sell those drills, you must decide who it is you are trying to reach and then tailor your appeals suitably.

A resume service is even more to the point. The benefit of a good resume is a good job offer or a number of job offers from which one may choose the best one. Actually, resumes do not help people get jobs—not directly. Hardly ever does a resume produce a job offer. What it produces, if it works at all, is an invitation to be interviewed. *That*, the interview, brings a job offer if it is successful. So it is more to the point to explain that invitation as the benefit of having a good resume.

But the invitation isn't really the point, either. The true benefit is always the true goal of the customer, which is indeed the job. Thus the promise is that of job offers, and the "proof" is that the resumes you write produce interviews.

Helping customers see that the true objective of a resume is winning interviews that will result in job offers makes your appeal different and persuasive because it reflects greater insight into the entire job-finding process, while still featuring the real benefit of job offers. The other goodies—many choices of type and format, for example—are features to be mentioned as other reasons to patronize your resume service, but they are not benefits.

I learned that lesson when I sold services in developing winning proposals. As long as my promise was of better proposals and better proposal guidance, the response to my appeals was lukewarm. It got considerably hotter when I made the promise of helping the customer win contracts. That was what the customer really wanted, and that was the promise that warmed prospects' hearts and loosened their purse strings.

Paul A. built up his little printing business by selling a benefit without realizing it. He happened to have great knowledge not only of printing but of relevant editorial processes, and his customers soon learned that Paul could guide them in preparing their work for printing. They came to rely on him, and without Paul ever realizing it, it was his editorial know-how, not his printing service nor his prices, that brought him a steady stream of repeat business and new customers who were being referred to him.

Paul added great value to his printing services by the extra help he gave his customers without ever recognizing that he was doing that—adding value. Anyone can do that, however. Although large companies do it through advertising and major promotional campaigns, anyone, including you, can do the same thing via deliberate planning and activities. We are going to discuss these in the next chapter.

Chapter 3

Using Market Perceptions To Enhance Your Value

Value, like truth, is what we perceive it to be, and when the perception is firm enough, it becomes unshakeable. But it is not a matter to be left to chance: We must manage customer perceptions by first offering maximum value and then educating the customer to perceive that value as truth.

Sticker Shock

Everyone in business, and especially anyone in any kind of custom service business, becomes familiar with what is today referred to as "sticker shock." The term derives from the automobile salesrooms, where dealers are required by law to display the prices of their cars by a sticker fixed to a window. The "sticker" is a detailed listing of the various features, their costs and the bottom line or selling price of the car overall. It becomes the dash of cold water on a potential sale when a prospective customer looks at the sticker and the enormity of the price begins to penetrate the prospect's consciousness. The price is inevitably more, far more, than the prospect anticipated—inflation always seems to outrun our expectations and even our worst fears. It sends shock waves through the salesperson, as well as through the prospect, because the seller observes the prospect's reaction to the sticker, the all too obvious shock. One does not need a stun gun; the sticker does the job nicely.

This not-so-phenomenal phenomenon of sticker shock is often even more common to a service business than to a product-based enterprise because the cost of labor has accelerated even more rapidly and to a greater degree than the cost of things. Thus, the stunner occurs at the point where the customer inquires as to what your service will cost. In fact, it is worse in the custom service business because in an automobile showroom, the customer may view the sticker in advance, whereas in a custom service business the customer cannot learn the price until you have agreed on what needs to be done for the customer. Ergo, your quotation comes without warning. (It ought not, however, come without preamble, which is one of those subjects we shall be discussing later in examining ways to lessen the impact of sticker shock.)

You may dread that point in the discussion—where the customer asks the price—because you anticipate that the customer will undergo that price shock quite visibly—a reasonable premise, of course. You fear that the customer will express that shock quite unmistakably and may abandon the idea of doing business with you, so that the result is loss of the sale. Means for coping successfully with this sales problem (for it is a sales problem) will be discussed later when we address that and related problems in a chapter devoted to the ways and means of getting your price and getting paid. That chapter will address ways and means of presenting the price to the customer in such a way as to minimize the shock and make the unpleasant news more palatable. For now, however, let's address some specific means for helping customers perceive the true value of your services and so develop at least a bit of armor against sticker shock.

Antisticker Shock Measures

Sticker shock is greatest when it is a sudden disillusionment. The customer has a grossly inaccurate idea of what the cost would be, possibly based on wishful thinking, and the bad news arrives without preparation or conditioning of any kind as a true dash of cold water. This is the result of the customer having had nothing upon which to base an opinion of value. Sometimes the customer is thinking wishfully, but often the problem is that the customer's views have been distorted by the bait-and-switch advertising of some of your competitors.

For example, a resume-writing service may advertise, in quite bold print, a $9 resume. Obviously, to those of us who know something about the costs of doing business, $9 hardly pays for typing and laser printing a master copy of the resume, much less designing, formatting, editing and otherwise developing a quality product, even at minimum cost. But to the average customer, who may never have had a resume prepared before, $9 may seem to be a reasonable sum to pay for a one-page resume.

Obviously, you cannot undertake to educate the entire world in what it takes to produce a good-quality resume. You can, however, take measures to make clear what you offer, demonstrating the quality to help customers adopt the proper perception of the value of what you offer.

Only this morning I tried something new. Pressed for time, I was reluctant to visit the dealer's service shop to have my oil changed and lubrication checked because that invariably consumes at least a half-day of my time. I decided to try one of those specialty shops that promise a 15-minute lubrication and oil change. It was a branch of a national chain of "Grease 'n' Go" shops.

I was most impressed. I drove up and was immediately approached by a courteous young man with a clipboard who was briskly all-business. He asked a handful of questions, which he recorded on a form: Model year of my car, service I wanted, last name, address. He told me what the price would be, that they would get to my car in 10 minutes and that the service would require about 15 minutes.

I went across the street for a cup of coffee and came back about 20 minutes later. They were just closing the hood of my car, and in a few minutes their computer and printer clacked along, printing out a report that stated exactly what had been done and what that cost me. Although I had gone in for an oil change and general lubrication, I found that they had checked my tire pressure and all my fluids, added water to my windshield washer reservoir, sprayed the chassis, checked the antifreeze and reported the lowest temperature it was ready for, and washed my headlamps and the exterior of my windows, all without charge as routine courtesies.

The extra touches cost the shop little to do, I am sure, but they made an impressive list on the invoice, and I did appreciate them. I am at an age when I am reluctant to raise the hood of my car to check on things or crawl around checking my tires, so I would neglect these chores. It's a great comfort to have somebody do them for me.

My dealer also did all of this for me, of course, but at a much higher cost in both time and money. How can I now go anywhere else but "Grease 'n' Go" for my oil changes and lubrication? They have made a new customer for the services they provide, despite my loyalty to my dealer for other maintenance.

Suppose now that you were to adopt this idea in your resume business. You would advertise the extra services and list them in your invoice at no charge. They might include extra copies of the resume, laser printed; computer spelling and grammar check; a list of employers in the area, with addresses and telephone numbers; a special discount or dollars-off coupon for some additional service, such as a transmittal letter; a handout of job-hunting tips; and perhaps other items you can find. You can probably automate these extra services so that they cost you little, but that isn't the point. They are extras, and they are free—courtesies. That means a great deal to most customers.

Packaging: In the Most Profound Sense

You will recall that with some products, such as cosmetics and perfume, I pointed out that the package often costs more than its contents. You might even say, with considerable justice, that the vendor is selling the package, rather than what is in it. Certainly, the package is responsible to a large degree for the customer's impressions and, therefore, perception of value.

That discussion referred to the literal or *physical* packaging—the perfume bottle, the lipstick tube, the compact, the jewelry case and other such containers. The containers themselves enhanced the perceived value of the products. A customer is immediately impressed highly by what is obviously a costly and unique package that was designed with great care and specifically for the product. When I bought a small circuit board to enlarge the memory of my printer, it arrived nested precisely in a case that one might justifiably expect to enclose a costly bracelet or necklace: It looked very much like such a package. It made me feel a great deal better about paying nearly $100 for a very small circuit board holding only a few small chips.

No matter how sophisticated one is, one can hardly help having his or her perception affected by such refinements as this. It inevitably suggests that the product contained therein is deemed by the manufacturer to be of great value, justifying great expense and care in packaging. That alone lends a perceived value to the item that has no relationship to its intrinsic value or actual cost to create. The packaging is a reflection of what the seller thinks is the value of the item, and it thus suggests that value to the customer.

Packaging, however, especially when used in a marketing sense, goes far beyond the matter of physical containers. It refers to all the measures and methods adopted to create an impression, often a first impression, but also a lasting one. It refers to the creation and maintenance of an image. It refers to the difference between arriving at an important social event in a taxi or in a chauffeur-driven limousine; the difference between being well turned-out and looking shabby and indifferent; the difference between a store on Fifth Avenue and one on Second Avenue. An individual struggling to succeed as an entertainer will go hungry in order to dress well—to be packaged appropriately. One young man, still in the early years of his career, told me that he had spent far more money than he could afford to have a most expensive suit tailored for him, to be worn only on those special occasions when he felt it necessary to present an unmistakable image of success and a sense of great self-confidence. Not only did he *look* successful when he wore that special suit, he told me, but he *felt* successful: It changed his self-perception. He felt like an equal when he dealt with others, even when interviewing for a new job, and that always came across to the others.

This is a most important idea. How you feel about yourself somehow comes across to others, and it affects your apparent worth. It is unfailingly true that you cannot convince others of anything you do not yourself believe. That absolutely critical quality of perseverance—"hanging in there," as we so often put it today—is the consequence only of believing in yourself and what you are trying to accomplish. Call it faith, call it positive thinking or call it self-confidence, if you will; it amounts to the same thing: You believe in you.

Packaging, in the greater sense, is something you always do in marketing whatever it is that you sell, whether you do it consciously or unconsciously. You can allow your image to just happen—develop spontaneously by doing nothing about it and thinking not at all about it—or you can plan and manage it. Allowing it to happen spontaneously—by chance, that is—means that you have no control over it at all. Packaging is whatever the customer sees, feels and believes about you and what you offer, the image you present.

I recall the dentist I went to when I was a youngster. He had a shabby little office above a cigar store at a busy intersection in West Philadelphia, and treatment of any kind was invariably a dollar a visit. Much later in life I went to a dentist who maintained a suite of offices in a modern office condominium, with a comfortable, well-furnished waiting room in which music played softly in the background that was visited every few minutes by a dental hygienist in a spotless white uniform who arrived to usher the next patient into the inner offices. Of course, services here cost far more than a dollar a visit.

Packaging What *You* Do

You may be skeptical about all this or reluctant to accept it as something that applies to you. That is not an unusual reaction. Or you may agree partially but without real understanding. (We will get to that problem too, eventually.) You may simply be wondering how this applies to you, or you may have begun to raise objections mentally to the whole idea. Perhaps you are convinced that all this refers to mere "front" or window dressing that cannot seriously affect the prices you can command. You may believe that your business is "different," that it isn't sensitive to such matters as packaging and image. You may agree philosophically with the importance of packaging and image, but only for "the other guy," not for you. For what you do, it doesn't matter much, it's too expensive, it doesn't really apply to your kind of business, and there is no way you can make it work for you, anyway.

We've been talking about what others do. Now let's talk about *you* and how these ideas might help you make your own business venture a great deal more profitable. Be prepared now for apparent paradoxes or inconsistencies: The discriminations between what makes for helpful packaging and what is simply ostentatious and perhaps even in bad taste can be fairly subtle.

Understanding Mistaken Image Issues

In my experience, most individuals venturing into a business enterprise are not unconscious of image and its importance. They do tend to concern themselves with it to some degree, at least in such matters as the following (but often do not think beyond these items):

- An impressive business name
- Expensive stationery
- An elaborate brochure
- A custom-designed logo
- A prestige address
- Costly office furniture

All of these are intended to create an impression of size, success and importance, and they can contribute to such impressions.

But they can also backfire when they are not handled skillfully. Let us consider each of these:

An Impressive Business Name

Unfortunately, too many budding entrepreneurs confuse size with quality: They adopt lengthy names believing that customers will be impressed by such grand names as "Continental Digital Information Services Corporation." However, it may have the reverse effect. As one executive observed to me one day, with an amused smile, "I find that the bigger the name, the smaller the company."

In fact, look at the utter simplicity of the names of many great corporations:

- International Business Machines (IBM)
- General Electric Company (GE)
- Radio Corporation of America (RCA)
- General Motors Corporation (GMC)
- American Telephone and Telegraph (AT&T)
- Standard Oil (ESSO)
- U.S. Steel (USS)
- General Foods
- Chrysler Corporation
- Ford Motor Corporation
- Western Union

Not only are the names quite direct and simple, but they usually provide at least some definition of, or at least a clue to, what the organization is about. Remember that each of these great corporations began as a small business that managed to survive and grow. Obviously, a grandiose name is not a necessity for success. In fact, the understatement of a direct and simple name, such as these, signals quiet self-confidence that is somehow more impressive than lengthy names that are quite obviously intended to impress by overwhelming people. Such names often come off to observers as bluster or as at least trying to lay down something of a smoke screen.

Cryptic names are also a wasted effort. Some entrepreneurs devise cryptic names, such as Twilight Zone Associates or Ones and Zeros, which was referred to in Chapter 2, that give no clue to the nature of what the business offers customers. A business name is somewhat like the headline of an advertisement or the title of a book in at least this respect: Even when it is lucid and easily understandable, only one in five of those who see and read a headline or title go on to read whatever text follows it. A leading objective of a headline or title is to arouse interest and persuade those who read it to want to know more. Perhaps the mysterious-sounding headline or title may do that occasionally, but the headline or title with a clear message is far more dependable.

Expensive Stationery

It is quite common for beginners in business to believe that they must have obviously costly letterheads, envelopes and business cards in matching sets, even to the excessive degree of having all embossed. This, they hope, will overwhelm prospective customers and ensure sales.

There are hazards in this. In printing, the bulk of the cost is up front in preparation so that it costs almost as much to print 500 pieces of stationery as to print 5,000 pieces. The economic principle known as the "economy of scale" (the decline in unit costs with large quantity) is busily at work in printing. Ergo, there is great pressure to buy in large quantity when you buy expensive printing of any sort, whether it is stationery, brochures or other materials.

One quite common hazard is that too often, a year or less after you have launched your new enterprise, your address, telephone number, business name or other items have changed, and you wonder what you are going to do with all those boxes of letterheads and envelopes.

Another hazard is the possibility of backfire. The evidence of costly appurtenances alarms some customers, leading to the impression that your services will be too costly. The factory worker with a grievance is not likely to call on the prestigious law firm with 150 lawyers in a high-rise office suite with a dozen secretaries and deep rugs but is likely to seek a lone wolf lawyer working from home or from a storefront office. They not only fear being confronted with costs they cannot manage, but they are thoroughly intimidated by the entire "prestige" scene and are sure that they cannot navigate successfully there.

In some cases, even those who are not at all intimidated by an overwhelming presence feel much more comfortable in surroundings that provide evidences of careful cost control and that so lend the hope the cost will be an affordable one.

In any case, it will never harm you or your image to use a good grade and good weight of plain white or off-white bond paper, printed tastefully with matching envelopes and business cards of similar design. Many suppliers can furnish these to you in modest quantities—e.g., 1,000 to 2,000 pieces—at competitive prices. Time enough later, when you are reasonably sure that you will not be making important changes, to consider the economy of quantity purchases of stationery and other things you believe you need.

In that context, here is a message from a computer consultant, Richard Hathway, who published it on the CompuServe electronic bulletin board and gave me his permission to quote him:

Do NOT rent the big office with the big executive desk.

Do NOT buy a fancy car!

Just get the business going using a used PC and fax machine stuck in a corner of your basement!

Above all do NOT borrow money to start the business!

Get some work first . . . the "I am a businessman" toys can come later!

Regards from,

Richard "who made these mistakes" Hathway

An Elaborate Brochure

You probably do need at least one general brochure. Most businesses do. As in the case of stationery, but to an even larger degree, you can easily go to costly and unnecessary extremes. At least in the early days of developing your business, you can do quite well with a simple brochure, printed on a good grade of paper. In brochures, as in stationery, there is an elegance in quiet, businesslike simplicity.

A Custom-Designed Logo

A logo, short term for logotype, is a symbol that identifies your business. It may be a stylized letter, a sketch or something quite arty. Note that, as in the case of company names, many large corporations use the simplest of logos, often the stylized initials of their company name. However, the main point here is that a logo, unlike a name and stationery, is not a business necessity. It is quite expensive to have one custom designed, and it really adds nothing of practical value to your business, especially in the early years when you are still struggling to get established. At that point, a customer may or may not remember you because your logo is distinctive; it would be an exception and, even then, it would probably not benefit you. As in the case of the banker who will lend you money only when you can prove that you don't need it, the distinctive logo is a tangible asset only when you have reached the point where you do not need it.

A Prestige Address

Unlike the logo or the stationery, your business address may be important, depending on the nature of your business. If your business depends on most of your customers visiting you, home-basing your business is quite likely to be impractical. You probably then need a commercial address: You must then think of the convenience of your customers, for one thing; never underestimate the power of convenience in motivating customers. In many businesses, however, a prestigious location is even more important than a convenient location, and it is of great importance to success. The customer's confidence in you is never unimportant, but it can be absolutely vital in some businesses. If you are a stockbroker or investment counselor, for example, a shabby office in a threadbare neighborhood is not likely to inspire much confidence or attract a great many customers!

Despite that generalization, the importance of location is a variable, depending on the nature of what you do. If you are an independent professional of some sort—architect, engineer, psychologist, consultant or similar—and you are in pursuit of the "carriage trade," it can be important to have offices in a prestigious office building, one usually housing many other professional offices. On the other hand, even in a professional calling, your practice may be such that you generally visit your customers and find it viable to have your office in your own home. You may have an address problem nevertheless: You may prefer not to use your home address in your advertising and correspondence. Many home-based entrepreneurs choose, for that reason, to use a box number as a business address.

My own preference is for a box at the nearest post office. That may not be feasible for everyone, or you may prefer not to have it known that you use a post office box. Some have the notion that a post office box has a negative connotation for a business, although I have never found evidence to support this idea. An alternative is to use one of the many private mail drops who operate in a storefront setting. They will provide you with their street address and receive mail for you, and they usually offer a variety of other services that you may find useful, such as copying services, telephone answering, parcel wrapping and shipping. (Many "mailbox" services are also agents for parcel delivery and overnight services.)

Costly Office Furniture

If you must receive customers on your premises regularly, you will be concerned with the impression they get from the fixtures and furniture in your office. Once again, as in the case of the other matters we have just discussed, there are extremes, and the middle road is usually the best one. Use furniture a cut above orange crates, but you can almost surely stop short of solid mahogany and hand-rubbed finishes.

Strangely enough, things are often not what they seem, especially to nonexperts. The most expensive versions of many products are sometimes the cheapest-looking to the layperson. On one U.S. Air Force contract I was involved in professionally, the client was under some pressure from Congress for their alleged extravagances. The client therefore asked us to use the cheapest-looking paper and bindings we could find in printing their reports and manuals. We actually went to additional expense to get paper that looked cheap! In most of the foregoing areas, with a bit of care and good judgment, you can get products that actually appear to be of the highest class and yet are modestly priced.

The Impact on the Customer

If you somehow manage to persuade your customers, even unintentionally, that you use only the most costly supplies, furniture, fixtures and equipment, it will probably suggest to the customers that your services do not come cheaply. They will probably presume that your services are most likely to be high priced. That helps, to the extent that many people judge quality and value by the price and by the symbols of success. Still, for many other customers, that does not directly affect how they perceive the value of your services. They tend to perceive value only in terms of what you and your services do for them. For example, they *expect* to pay a specialist more than they pay a general practitioner, and they see it in their interest to do so for the privilege of receiving the specialist's services—if and when they recognize the specialist as offering services not available from a general practitioner or offering services of much greater skill and reliability than those of the generalist. The customer derives a sense of comfort and security from that perception, and that justifies a higher price. So you do want to display evidence of success, while you do not appear to be extravagant. It helps to do as lawyers and physicians do: They paper the walls of their waiting rooms and offices with innumerable framed certificates of achievements that attest to their education, skills, awards and professional recognition.

Motivation

Take note of the statement above that the customer derives a sense of comfort and security from the perception of special skills to be employed in his or her behalf, and that perception justifies a higher price. That sense of comfort and security also sums up the most important factor in this discussion: The emotional benefit. That is what really drives perceptions in judging value and making buying decisions, even when the judgments are not fully conscious ones. The need to feel comfortable and secure is a powerful need, as insurance companies certainly know, for they stress it quite commonly in their appeals. The one with the cupped hands makes the point of being in good hands with them rather effectively and then reinforces that notion with their logo. Another quite famous and familiar insurance underwriter essays to provide that sense of comfort by displaying the Rock of Gibraltar, a time-honored symbol of enduring immobility, as their logo, suggesting solid dependability. Providing the customer with a greater-than-usual sense of comfort and security is a benefit that customers will certainly perceive as value.

Convenience is a great motivator too. The "convenience stores" are well named because they provide just that, even if they charge a bit more than the supermarkets. You have the convenience of parking at the door, not hundreds of feet away across a great parking lot. You have the convenience of finding what you want within a few feet of the front door, not somewhere in the great recesses of a great store with many aisles and signs you must traverse and search.

How To Find or Create Value Enhancements

It is always possible to find or create value enhancements. In one case you may actually build something new and different into the product that makes it more valuable to the customer. In another case, the item is already there, waiting for you to discover it. Or perhaps you have always known of it but never considered ways of presenting it to the customer to make the greater value apparent. Consider this case:

> When I decided to try my hand at presenting a seminar on proposal writing, I considered what USP— Unique Selling Point—I could offer. That is, I wondered how I could specialize my seminar so that it offered something that was quite different, quite distinctive and of readily apparent greater value than what other seminars on proposal writing offered. I thought about it for some time. I considered what had been the chief cause of my own successes in proposal writing, for one: What had been my "secret weapon"?
>
> I decided that it was my ability to devise strategies. I had been long convinced that the most important single factor in proposal writing was the capture strategy, that grand plan that would win the customer over and enable me to surpass my competitors. I decided that the focal point of the seminar would be the teaching of strategy.
>
> I decided too that I needed something to make my seminar highly distinctive. I had earlier coined the term "Proposalmanship," but I did not think that strong enough to make my seminar truly distinctive in the sense of offering something not available elsewhere—not a USP, that is. I came to the conclusion that the seminar had to be characterized as advanced beyond its competitors, a graduate course, in fact. The brochure that resulted announced, in suitable type and layout, "Proposalman-

ship, the *graduate* course in winning government contracts through strategy."

My literature package was also different. Instead of the typical oversize brochure bulk mailed without an envelope, inviting itself to be discarded as "junk mail" without pausing to scan it even briefly, I used a sales letter and small brochure, mailed in a plain white envelope as first class mail and resembling nothing as much as it resembled normal business correspondence.

The results were highly satisfactory. There were several elements responsible for the success of the mailing, including several items presented in the outline that was included in the literature package. But the chief cause of its success was the "graduate course" characterization. That also added a degree of "class," supported by the first-class mailing (instead of the usual junk mail approach). This guaranteed that the envelope would be opened.

An error made by many entrepreneurs in their marketing is to take a polyfeature approach. They describe a litany of benefits and features under the theory that if you make enough promises, most customers will find something they like. Unfortunately, that is a flawed theory. It makes it all but impossible to see you as a specialist, for one thing. Dilution alone is a deadly flaw, but there is more: You have diluted your presentation so that it now has no focus, and focus is essential if you are to prove a point or make a firm impression of any kind. It is asking readers to search for the items that interest them, but they will not do that, of course. Customers do not sell themselves; you have to sell them.

Finding Focal Points

A key element in shaping perceptions of value is finding or identifying the key focal point. What is there about what you do or offer that is superior (to that of your competitors)? Or, alternatively, what can you do or offer to do that will make your service distinctive and somehow superior?

To find the elements for this you must do an organized analysis, and a worksheet is offered here to help you in this effort (Figure 3.1). The procedure suggested is to find the words to describe the principal function of your service in a brief, summary form, using just key words: Verbs and nouns. (Avoid adjectives and adverbs.) Because that may or may not be easy for you to do, the form offered here provides a number of lines. If your service is a highly specialized one, it may be relatively easy for you to describe your service. But if it is somewhat generalized, you may have some difficulties summarizing it in a single statement. Or it may be that your services are so diverse that each has to be marketed independently of the others. In that case, select just one service for this

Figure 3.1   **Worksheet: What My Service Does**

Summary description: _____

_____

1. Major functions/benefits:

_____
_____
_____
_____
_____
_____
_____

2. Secondary functions/benefits:

_____
_____
_____

3. Special features:

_____
_____
_____
_____

4. Notes

_____
_____

exercise and repeat it later for each of your other services. In my own case, for example, I might do such an exercise for proposal consulting, another for copywriting and still another for ghostwriting as the only practical way to describe the diverse set of services I am prepared to deliver to clients. There are far too many problems and difficulties in selling them all in a single presentation.

The Importance of Viewpoint

There is a "catch" here. On the face of it, it seems simple enough to describe your service. The problem is that you will probably describe your service as *you* see it, if you do not make a deliberate and conscious effort to avoid that trap. What you need is a description of your service as your customers see it.

The two views rarely come even close to matching. Each of you tends to see your offering in terms of your personal interests. You see it as something you sell at a profit. Your customers try to see your offering in what's-in-it-for-me terms. Perhaps they can answer the what's-in-it-for-me question for themselves, but most often they need help. Certainly, it is in your interest to help them see you in the terms that interface with your own interests. They might see a proposal-writing service as their personal escape from the task of writing. But that is not nearly so motivating for your purposes as their seeing it as a surer route to contracts.

To ferret out provocative motivators for your customers, ask yourself not only why they would or should use such a service, but what are the benefits they derive, and then what is the most important benefit—their reasons for wanting a proposal at all, regardless of how and where they get it. Are they willing to pay for better-written proposals for the sake of owning better-written proposals? Of course not; they want to win contracts. They pay you to write proposals for them because, they believe, it will help them to win those contracts they are after or to win grants, in the case of grant proposals.

That is true in every case. What the customer buys from you is something that will help him or her gain and enjoy some benefit.

It may not be even a conscious or deliberately rationalized goal, but one the customer "feels" a desire for. A customer may go to some trouble to patronize a given store for the pleasure of being recognized by name and warmly greeted by a congenial merchant who has become almost a personal friend. The more you understand your customers' motivations, the easier it is to understand their perceptions and to work to shape them favorably.

Identifying Major Benefits

It is for this reason that several lines in the form are offered for your choices. The idea is to consider more than one benefit and possible motivation, as well as to give you the opportunity to revise and polish your statement, trying to approach the goal of greater insight into the customer's motivations. That will help you achieve the ultimate goal of pinning down the benefit most important to the customer so that you may focus efforts on addressing that motivation and finding ways to increase the benefit. Consider, for example, how you might develop functional descriptions if you were some kind of computer consultant:

Summary description: Computer training services
Major functions/benefits:
Installation and training
Teaching software use and operation
Making customers capable in computers
Giving customers confidence in computer use
Increasing customer's employable skills
Helping customers win higher-paying jobs
Helping customers win promotions
Helping customers make more money
Helping customers enjoy the better things in life

Note that the descriptions are increasingly worded to describe the ultimate benefit that customers could achieve. The first items are what *you do*. The final items are what *the customer gets* as a result of what you do. They are also increasingly emotional stimuli. They are the promises that arouse the desire to buy from you at your price. And, of course, price resistance is in inverse proportion to the customer's perception of value and motivation: The more eager the customer is to buy, the less he or she resists what he or she might otherwise consider to be a high price.

Finding Secondary Benefits and Special Features

There could be secondary benefits, such as learning how to play computer games, being "in" about computers with one's friends or realizing other relatively minor benefits. In fact, this might be the prime motivator for some customers, but the benefit to their careers would be far more commonly the primary and more powerful motivation. Featuring the secondary benefits might produce a few extra customers, but you ought not to dilute the power of your appeal by weakening the perception of value that would be inherent in the promise of the primary benefit of greater career success.

Special features might be anything that would produce secondary benefits, such as keyboard templates or other devices to aid learning, some form of free consultation following the completion of a training program, a certificate of completion and competency, a lesson or two in basic computer maintenance, a training manual that would do service later as a reference manual, or almost any other add-on.

In deciding what the major benefit is, you must consider the customer you are pursuing: The benefits are not necessarily the same for all classes or kinds of customers. Those listed here would be appropriate for the training services delivered directly to most individual customers. But suppose you wanted to market these services through computer dealers, as well as directly. What benefits would you offer the dealers to employ you to deliver your services to their customers or otherwise direct customers to you?

The dealer's motivation is primarily to sell computer hardware and software, and that would normally be the prime benefit for you to promise: The boost in sales your service would provide the dealer. A secondary benefit would be the additional profit a dealer might gain by selling your services for a commission or at a discount of some sort, or perhaps the benefit of cooperative advertising and mutual referrals.

Suppose that you also wish to market these services to employers who would pay for the training of their employees. How would you appeal to employers—i.e., what benefits could you promise?

The obvious benefits an employer might look for would be increases in employee efficiency. You would need some argument here to demonstrate that it is more effective to have you train the employees than to have them learn on the job. Or you might argue that even employees who are supposedly already well qualified in advance as a condition of employment often are not, or they are at least not well trained in the special working methods you teach. You might, in fact, find that latter the most important promise, that your service is not to teach fundamentals but to teach advanced methods for greatest efficiency. (Refer to the "graduate" course in proposal writing described a few pages ago.) The USP approach is always a powerful one, if handled skillfully and honestly: You must, in fact, deliver something special if you promise to do so.

Creating the USP

There is also the consideration of competition and how it affects you and what you can or should promise. It is when you are facing strong competition—e.g., a dozen others who offer computer training—that you most need a USP. And here one recalls the case of a beer company who ran a major advertising campaign in which they featured the promise, with appropriate illustrations, "Our bottles are sterilized with live steam," thus assuring their customers that the content of their bottles was uncontaminated.

The practice of sterilization with live steam was not unique at all but was quite a common practice. However, no competitor had ever used this as an advertising or marketing promise (and none would now say, "me too") so the public had no way of knowing that it was not unique. It was, therefore, a USP, as far as the public was concerned. In fact, many shrewd marketers create USPs in this manner. The USP, if it is impressive enough, makes your service itself unique and therefore with a value all its own.

As a result of your decisions as to the customers you wish to pursue and your analyses of the nature of the competition you face, you may very well need to develop more than one worksheet, perhaps even several: You probably will have to market differently for different market segments—to different kinds of customers, that is—if you want to command the best prices.

A Major Spin-Off Benefit

We have spent many words here to discuss ways to shape customers' perceptions of value so as to enable you to get higher prices for what you sell. The intention here is to analyze ways to increase the actual value of what you sell, not to maneuver customers into paying more than what you sell is worth.

The increase in actual value is a benefit that accrues to you as a result of doing the analyses suggested here. In developing arguments for valuing your services above those of your competitors, you are doing more than developing more effective advertising and marketing materials, although that is a direct objective of the efforts. You are, in fact, finding the means to actually make your service a superior one that can command higher prices by the simple objective virtue of being worth more. You begin to think of your business in terms of what it does for your customers, the direct benefits it delivers, and how you can magnify those benefits. This approach shapes your business itself, as well as how you advertise and market it. That is how great businesses are born, according to many leading founders of great companies, such as the late Ray Kroc (McDonald's) and Sam Walton (Wal-Mart).

Time To Look at the Numbers

We have been talking more or less philosophically about the influences and various considerations in setting your rates and making them both profitable and palatable to customers. For the most part, these have been considerations of marketing and sales promotion. But there is another consideration that is at least equally important: The dollars-and-cents side of your business. It's time now to get down to some specifics—hard numbers—that represent the harsh realities of business or "the facts on the ground," as some military people have put it. We'll begin to do that in the next chapter.

Chapter 4

Mastering the Financials

You are not going to become an accountant as a result of reading this chapter or this book, nor will you be expected to understand all about accounting or even be familiar with all its terms. (It has its argot, as all specialized fields do.) You should, however, understand and appreciate some basics of managing accounts that will enable you to gain a truer insight into your business than you would otherwise enjoy.

Why You Need To Understand the Rationale of Accounting

In this chapter you will not be confronted with or asked to master the many specialized concepts of formal accounting systems set up for and used by trained, professional accountants in business organizations. You will probably never need to cast your own balance sheets or profit and loss statements, or even to prepare other of your own financial statements and tax returns. In any case, the details of those activities are matters outside our concerns here.

Note, for example, how this introductory paragraph was titled. It did not promise to teach you the basics of accounting or suggest a need to know them. You do, however, need to understand those basic accounting ideas that are and should be important to you as a manager and proprietor, if not as an accountant. That is, you need to understand the accounting basics in lay terms—in everyday English. This is not to criticize or condemn the use of special accounting jargon, an idiomatic language both important and useful to accountants. You, however, need to understand accounting as a manager and proprietor, and that requires translating accounting into everyday English.

Most of all, you need to know why you need to keep accounts, why you *must* keep accounts even if you never post your own ledger, although I will encourage you to keep your own books: It is a simple task for the owner of a small business, and it encourages in you the development of a consciousness of fiscal management. The tax man cometh, and he wants to see your books or at least the figures you get from your books. But you do not keep books merely to satisfy his desires. You have an accounting system primarily to help you manage your business effectively—or you should have it for that major purpose. As we probe the subject in this chapter, you will begin to see why management of any business today, even the tiniest one, relies on accurate and up-to-date accounts.

The principles that explain the *why* of accounting are simple logic, when the esoteric jargon is stripped away and the principles are presented in simple language. I so present the facts of managing the money involved in conducting your business because I am not an accountant but only an experienced businessman.

You neither need nor should ever again simply accept what your accountant says without understanding exactly what your accountant is trying to convey to you, so that you are fully enabled to agree or disagree with your accountant's message. Accounting manipulations and jargon may become arcane, but the basics of income, direct costs and indirect costs are simple concepts every business owner is entirely capable of understanding. It is most difficult, if not impossible, to understand them if you are handicapped by not having an understanding of such related matters and terms as overhead, fringe benefits, payables, receivables, depreciation and amortization. Deplorable as it may be, therefore, we must examine these matters. But perhaps the following anecdote will help you appreciate the significance of this.

Accounting: Why Do We Need It?

An uncle of mine was an upholsterer and furniture refinisher back in the simpler time of the 1930s, when I was a youngster observing this without understanding it at that time. His was a small business. In fact, it was a classic form of home-based business, because he had a shop in a neighborhood retail location with living quarters behind and above the storefront. (That was a rather common thing for neighborhood businesses in those days, and it still exists to some extent in older urban neighborhoods.) As a one-man business, he hired help only on a temporary or subcontract basis when he happened to get a job that was too big for him to do alone or he had become too busy to undertake another job and did not want to turn a customer away and so risk losing both the customer and the sale. He kept his records in a five-cent notebook and his bills and receipts in a cigar box, a handy and widely used receptacle in those times, where he stored all his receipts and copies of his bills. (He probably had never heard the term *invoice*; he received and sent out *bills*.)

There was no Social Security tax and no withholding tax yet, in the early 1930s, although they were coming in the not-very-distant future. (Those who earned more than $1,000 a year were taxed on their income and paid the tax at the end of the year. (The first year I had to pay it, I was taxed a sum less than $3.) Many millions of Americans did not make more than $1,000 a year and paid no income tax. Those who did pay any significant amount of income tax were relatively affluent. In that simpler time, a simple business owner, operating a simple business, did not need a complex system of accounting to pay the taxes due and know exactly what was what about his or her business from day to day. It was a time when one could fly a small business by the seat-of-the-pants—instinctual—method.

Even today the law does not really require you to have a system more complex than that. It requires only that you keep records, and it is up to you to decide how you will do so. But in today's complex structure of taxes and reporting requirements, it would be unwise to rely on a notebook and cigar box as the repository of your business records. You would probably find it difficult to *understand* your business as you should. You would have trouble simply keeping track of the income and expenses of the business and even greater difficulty in managing it. Today, you need something a bit more sophisticated than a notebook and cigar box full of records to qualify even minimally as an accounting *system.*

In spite of that, and perhaps contrary to popular belief, it is not for the IRS that you keep records and a formal accounting system. As far as the IRS and your taxes are concerned, you could manage a one-person service business with that notebook and cigar box; you need only to have records, if and when the IRS challenges your tax returns. But you need to *manage* your business, and you will want to arrange your affairs to minimize the taxes for which you are liable legally. An accounting system can help you with that, as a cigar box full of papers cannot. Ultimately, as we proceed, you will see why that is so. But here is a little personal experience that illustrates in simple terms one important reason for having an organized accounting system, no matter how simple or small your business:

Smitty, a friend who was an independent TV serviceman, and I were having lunch one day at a favorite neighborhood restaurant where we met often to chat and exchange news and information. During our conversation, in discussing the state of business in general, he remarked to me that he found the running of a successful business a simple manner.

"Whatever it pays you to do, keep doing," he advised me. "Whatever doesn't pay you, stop doing."

"Easy for you to say," I retorted.

We grinned at each other, fully understanding each other: What Smitty had said was easy for anyone to say but not so easy to do, as he knew quite well. We both knew that it isn't always easy to know which of your activities are profitable and which are not profitable, especially when your accounting system does not give you the numbers on a continuing basis and in a manner that makes trends and aberrations highly visible. The problem is probably most acute in many large corporations. Consequently, in large organizations, losing operations often go on for years before corporate management recognizes the situation and gives some attention to doing something about it. Many organizations support unprofitable divisions for one reason or another.

However, that kind of thing is certainly not peculiar to large corporations. You would be quite surprised at how easily you can be deceived about which activities are the winners and which the losers in your own small business, if you do not have established mechanisms designed to keep you informed—i.e., to give you an accurate and up-to-date profile of your business operations, to give you a *measure*, so that you do not rely on your instinct or "gut feeling," which is notoriously unreliable at delivering bad news.

Suppose, for example, that your business involves several distinct services that you offer your customers: Let us suppose that you maintain and repair computers, you train people in computer use, you advise your customers on what to buy when they need new equipment and you install networks when customers have several computers and want them linked together to share printers, modems and other peripheral components. However, you keep general records of your business income and expenses, without separating it by the kind of services for which you are paid.

You may be able to determine that you are turning a profit overall, but do you know whether all your services are profitable? Perhaps one service is so profitable that it covers up losses you suffer from another service that is really highly unprofitable. That is certainly not an unusual situation: I was once an executive of one division in a corporation with 12 divisions, where one was breaking even, ten were losing money and one extremely profitable division was supporting them all. It can happen easily enough in even the small organization, if you do not provide the means to prevent losses from remaining hidden.

You may lose money on some tasks because you do not charge enough—because you cannot charge enough, because you cannot do those tasks efficiently or because some other factor prevents you from making those tasks profitable. In brief, your circumstances may make it impossible for you to do some things profitably, even if a competitor can do them at a profit because your competitor has much different circumstances, such as lower labor costs or some special asset.

As an example of that, a small company in the Virginia suburbs of Washington responded to a request for proposals (RFP) from a major government contractor in Idaho. The contractor wanted a training program written and completed on an unusually tight schedule, one that appeared all but impossible to satisfy. However, it so happened the company had data and materials on the shelf that were very close to what the client wanted. That gave this small company a great advantage over its competitors. The company was able to submit a low bid, meet the impossible schedule requirement and do the job at a reasonable profit because of its peculiar advantage over competitors.

That is an individual case, although not a highly unusual one. But the principle applies in general: It explains exactly why many businesses choose to specialize, concentrating their efforts in some area where they have an advantage over competition by reason of some specific experience, special interest, special "contacts" or other circumstance that gives them an edge. That, too, is why you need that proper accounting system. It may guide you in choosing an area in which to specialize, but even if it does not do that, it gives you a constant appreciation of how your business is doing and answers some important questions you should be asking of your accounting records. It also helps you determine the areas in which specialization would be of greatest advantage to you. (In fact, some entrepreneurs use this as a planned guide to finding the most profitable area(s) in which to specialize.) Your accounting system ought to provide you answers to such questions as the following:

- What services show me the greatest volume of sales?
- What services are the most profitable?

- What services show me the smallest volume of sales?
- What services are the least profitable?
- What services produce the bulk of the total income?
- What services produce a minimal portion of the income?
- Which are the greatest expenses?
- What is my overhead?
- How do various types of expenses relate to each of the above?
- Is my price structure the realistic one—i.e., do I charge enough for what I do?

It is the answers to these and many other such questions that guide you in deciding not only what you must charge, but what to continue and discontinue doing. That is, the answers to these questions give rise to a second set of questions about an individual service or product, such as these:

- Is it possible to make this service profitable?
- Should I raise the price for this service?
- Can I raise the price without losing customers?
- Can I reduce the costs of providing this service?
- Can I perform this service more efficiently?
- Should I continue this service as is, combine this service with another or discontinue it?

All of this rationale applies to the services you provide, of course, but not only to those. That rationale ought to apply also to the investments you make and to the running or daily expenses. You need to know, for example, which of your advertising expenditures are viable—produce worthwhile results—and which are largely wasted. The same thing goes for your public relations and other promotional activity. I can guarantee you that if you do not check the facts but rely on those often misleading "gut feelings" (which are, unfortunately, heavily tainted by wishful thinking) you will continue to waste money on unproductive advertising and other wasteful marketing activity. A price you charge may be as high as your competitors' prices and yet be too low for profit because associated costs are unnecessarily high. You may not be able to judge whether a price is right until and unless you determine whether associated expenses are necessary or unnecessary or an advertising campaign may not produce enough business to justify its existence.

Those in mail order or direct mail marketing believe in testing every important element of an offer before "rolling out"—committing to a complete campaign, which would normally involve many thousands or hundreds of thousands of pieces mailed or great sums invested in advertising programs. Figures 4.1 and 4.2 illustrate the types of forms used to record and evaluate mailing campaigns. The three sample forms of Figure 4.1 are for the recording of actual sales and calculating the return on investment, which is the main objective. However, other items of data are also interesting and useful. In addition to actual dollars, it helps to know what the ratios—percentages—are.

Figure 4.2 is a form used to record and evaluate responses to a campaign soliciting inquiries—to prospect for sales leads and to build mailing lists of one's own.

For campaigns that rely on media advertising, a slightly different form is required, although the purpose and the strategy is the same: To record and evaluate results by measuring several parameters—e.g., number of sales, average size of sale (if that is a variable), return on investment in dollars and cost per order. Figure 4.3 is a form for recording the results of print advertising in various periodicals. Several variables are measured, as you can see.

The same philosophy is pursued in the form of Figure 4.4, which records and evaluates the results of broadcast advertising on radio and TV.

Finally, Figure 4.5 is a form for comparing the results among various media—print, radio, TV and any others you might use.

The forms or worksheets shown here are typical and reflect the general "tracing" idea. You may, of course, use these or design your own forms and worksheets. These were designed especially

***Figure 4.1* Forms for Recording and Evaluating Responses to Campaign Soliciting Sales**

Key: _____ Day & Date: _____

Day, Date	Key	Mailing Date	Number Pieces	Cost	Number Orders	Sales ($)
	Totals:					

Key: _____ Number Pieces Mailed: _____ Date: _____ Cost: $ _____

Number Orders	Response %	Sales ($)	Fulfillment Cost	Return on Investment %	Gross Profit

Key: _____ Date of Mailing: _____ Cost Per Lead: _____

Date	Number Sales	Sales Total ($)	Remarks
Totals:			Cost Per Sale: $_____

***Figure 4.2* Form for Recording and Evaluating Responses to Campaign Soliciting Inquiries**

Key: _____ Date Mailed: _____ Cost: _____

Date	Number Calls	Number Cards/Letters	Notes
Totals:			Cost Per Inquiry: $ _____

Figure 4.3 Form for Recording Results of Print Advertising

Day & Date: _____

Key	Periodical	Issue Date	Cost	Number Orders	Sales ($)
		Totals:			

Figure 4.4 Form for Recording Results from Radio/TV Commercials

Day & Date: _____

Station	Date(s) Time(s)	Cost ($)	Number Orders	Cost/Order	Profit (Loss)
	Totals:				

Figure 4.5 Form for Comparing Media

Day & Date: _____

Medium	Date(s)	Cost ($)	Number Orders	Cost/Order	Profit (Loss)
	Totals:				

for direct response types of marketing, but the methodology is adaptable to other kinds of marketing and business operations.

What is required is that you find or invent some means for tracing the sources of your sales so that you can make at least a reasonable estimate of the costs of getting your sales as a co-efficient of the effectiveness of advertising and promotional investments you make in pursuit of sales. If, for example, you run a special promotion, you should key it in some manner that connects it with the sales it produces. It may require actually asking each new customer how he or she heard of you, although there are many more subtle ways of gaining such information. If you use media advertising, it is easy enough to key each advertisement with a fictitious name (I often advised customers in my advertising to ask for "Mr. Murphy" to get a special discount, or some other special benefit, for example.)

I enter each new customer's name and address in a database, of course, with suitable notations that identify the source of the new customer, as nearly as I can identify it. If the initial contact by a new customer is an inquiry, rather than an order, I so note it. If it is an order, I record it so that when I hear from this customer again it takes me only a moment to look up whatever information I have in my files.

The ability to "identify" is most impressive to the customer. Not long ago my own wife bought something from the Home Shopping Club on TV, and she was so delighted with the product that she called to order one sent to her mother in Miami. Almost instantaneously, after she mentioned this, the woman on the other end of the line cited her mother's name and address and asked if that was correct. My wife was enormously impressed by this, as most customers would be. Her customer-loyalty index rose immediately!

The income and cost data you collect ultimately finds its way onto your books, of course, where it becomes the "official" data of your business. There it appears in summary form, telling you overall what activities are giving you a good return and which are not. The worksheets give you the details to pursue clues to good and bad activities.

The accounting system, backed by the recordkeeping and analysis you practice, is thus actually a management tool. For most of us, it is or should be the most important management tool because it looks into the heart of the business: What dollars are coming in and from where are they coming, and what dollars are going out and to where they are going. Obviously you need more dollars coming in than going out, if you are to survive. But you must also know *how much* more you need coming in than going out to provide for the future of your business and how to improve the ratio.

Large corporations have large accounting systems. They have elaborate systems of ledgers and journals, usually on computers today. Of course, as a small business, you do not need an elaborate system. If you want to keep your own books, you can do so easily in a paper system or on your personal computer with any of many simple software programs available. Actually, you do not need "books," as large corporations do, for your small business; one book will do it all, providing between one set of covers all the essentials of a day journal or diary and the ledgers or a small computer program as an equivalent.

You don't need to know anything about how your automobile works to operate it and to have it serviced, although you should certainly know that it needs oil, lubrication, antifreeze and a few other basics. Similarly, you do need to know the essential basics of money management and keeping accounts to operate your business successfully. That includes understanding what the fees and rates are that you should charge and many related matters, such as how to explain your fees to your clients and make your clients understand that they are the right rates—as much in the client's interest to pay as in your interests to charge.

Accounting principles are not complex when we strip away the jargon and examine them as simple logic—what we often call "common sense." They are easily understood if we start from the most basic idea of money in two columns, as in Figure 4.6: The money that comes in and the money that goes out. It may shock an accountant to reduce matters to that simple equation. The accoun-

Figure 4.6 Income versus Outgo

Income (Fees)	Outgo (Expenses)
Writing	Rent
Editing	Postage
Illustrating	Printing
Proofreading	Salaries
Composition	Taxes
Layout	Insurance
Etc.	Etc.

tant would tend to call that an oversimplification, which appears to be a capital offense to most professionals when anyone translates their language into everyday English, but it's easy enough to do. There is one important observation to be made here, however: The fact of paying out money does not mean that everything you spend is cost. When you buy inventory—e.g., merchandise you will sell—that is mere conversion of cash into an asset of equal value. When you buy supplies or small items of equipment, you are also simply converting your money to another form, an asset of equal value.

That does not mean that you do not ultimately charge your business for the items. They are, in the end, costs. They lose value because they are no longer new, and the older they get, the more value they lose. Capital items, such as equipment, vehicles, furniture and real estate are put on depreciation schedules, and you charge off a portion of their original cost each year until you have charged the entire cost off as a deduction.

There are exceptions. Smaller items of equipment can be "expensed" or charged off in the year of purchase, as you would supplies. So they are costs that are indeed felt immediately.

Note what may appear to be something of an anomaly here. What is an accounting truth is not necessarily a business truth. For example, many items you buy help you do your work more efficiently or enable you to offer services you could not offer before. In such cases, the money you spend is an investment, an expenditure representing cost that ought to bring back far more than it cost. I offer services today that I could not offer a year ago because I have equipment and software today that I did not have a year ago, and they have added capabilities I did not have before. Many of the accounting terms and practices that appear baffling to laypeople exist to handle such situations.

The Elements of Any Accounting System

There are two main elements necessary to a basic accounting system, the ledger and the diary or log, also referred to as a "day journal" or, simply, "journal." (Some accountants refer to postings in the day journal as "journalizing" the entries.) The ledger is where you post your receipts and expenditures by categories, as indicated in Figures 4.7 and 4.8. Some expenditure items will occur just once each month—rent and utility bills, for example—but others—postage and entertainment, for example—will be items that may occur many times during the month. But the form calls for the total postage and entertainment expenses for the month, so you have to collect each such item and post the total at the end of the month.

The same principle applies to your receipts or income. You record each receipt as it occurs and post the totals for each code at the end of the month. Thus you need to collect the many items during the month so that you have the total at the end of the month.

There are, of course, other elements in an accounting system, but these are the two principal elements and their functions you must appreciate to use your system well in managing your business. As you begin to study your postings, you will become ever more conscious of where your business stands, and you will begin to get answers to the questions posed a few paragraphs ago. Those are the answers that will enable you to manage your business for best results.

Figure 4.7   **Record of Receipts**

APEX Services: Receipts 1995

Month: _____	Total This Month	Total to Last Month	Total to Date
6010 Training Services			
6020 Repairs			
6030 Programming			
6040 Networking			
Miscellaneous			
TOTALS:			

Figure 4.8 **Record of Expenditures**

APEX Services: Expenditures 1995

Month: _____	Total This Month	Total to Last Month	Total to Date
8010 Accounting			
8020 Advertising/Marketing			
8030 Auto Expense			
8040 Books/Magazines/Subscriptions			
8060 Contributions			
8080 Health Insurance			
8080 Dental			
8090 Entertainment			
8100 Car/Office Insurance			
8120 Miscellaneous			
8130 Office Expense			
8140 Postage			
8150 Promotions/Gifts			
8160 Office Rent			
8170 Repairs			
8180 Payroll: Sher			
8180 Payroll: Herm			
8190 Subcontract			
8200 Supplies			
8220 Property Tax			
8230 Unemployment:			
IRS			
MD			
8240 Telephone Co./Cellular/Fax			
8250 Travel			
8300 MD Corp. Tax			
8310 FED Corp. Tax			
3050 IRS Withholding			
3060 SS/FICA/Med/WT			
3210 Computer/Credit Card			
Loans Repaid			
2010 Furniture/Fixtures			
5030 Nondeductibles			
8110 Interest Charges			
1020 Petty Cash			
1040 Receivable Loans			
TOTALS			

Where the Money Comes From

Money may come in from only one activity or type of activity—fees for one service or various services—or it may come in from other, additional activities—lectures, a newsletter, classes or others. Money goes out necessarily to several destinations: Rent or mortgage payments, telephone, transportation, postage, repairs, advertising, subscriptions, salaries, licenses and taxes, usually, and perhaps even more. (Yes, your own salary is not profit; seeing it as such is a common mistake of neophytes in business. Your salary is a cost item that "the business," an entity unto itself, must bear.)

A balance between the columns is necessary, as the minimum goal, but eventually there must be more income than outgo, if the business is to show a profit. And, as observed earlier, that balance must not be achieved at the cost of being unable to pay yourself a decent salary. Your salary or personal draw from your business is, by the way, a cost; it is not profit, not even gross profit. Be sure you understand that clearly: If you have decided that you ought to be able to pay yourself $750 per week, but you are unable to pay yourself more than $500 per week, you are subsidizing your own business by $250 per week. That is, in a real sense, a loss, although it is not a loss that you can write off as a business expense, unfortunately.

Profit and Loss: Are They Real?

You can often hear people who are in business, especially retailers, complain unremittingly that they are losing money. In many cases, it is a consistent and unending lament. Some will never admit, even grudgingly, to having made a profit. If pressed, they may say, with a shrug or resignation, "I manage to make a living."

One must wonder why they stay in business or, more to the point, how they are able to stay in business, much less "make a living," if they lose money every year.

One reason for this unchanging wail is superstition, the same superstition that makes the people of more than one culture present a humble and even self-deprecating facade (e.g., "This unworthy person," "Your humble servant," etc.). This false humility is a manifestation of the belief that the gods will punish anyone who displays excessive ego or sins by being too self-congratulatory. One must not offend the gods and invite disaster, runs this cultural superstition. It has become so ingrained in some cultures that the people almost instinctively use such expressions without an awareness of the original reasons for it, merely repeating it as a shibboleth.

That doesn't fully explain the matter, however. Not everyone who claims to be losing money is trying to avoid offending the gods or conforming to some cultural tradition. Many sincerely believe that they are losing money, although that may or may not be a fact in the strictest sense. "Losing money" is a highly flexible expression, meaning many things, according to the notions and standards of the individual. Some people moan that they lose money when a deal they expect does not materialize. What happens, in fact, is that they do not make the amount of money they had hoped and expected to make. Some people complain that they lose money when they made a smaller profit than they had at some previous time or smaller than they expected to realize. And for many the "loss" is a "paper loss," an accounting rationalization, and they are not out of pocket at all.

On the other hand, this behavior does not mean that there are no true losses in business or that proprietors do not often end a year with less money or fewer assets than those with which they started the year. That is, to put it into more dynamic terms, they operate below their costs, paying out more than they take in. That does happen too, and it is the kind of loss we want to talk about here first as one of the most common problems of small businesses struggling to survive. It is why the United States Small Business Administration and other organizations who analyze businesses often point to deficiencies in accounting as a major cause of small business failure: Many small business owners do not realize they are losing money because they do not have a complete understanding of or appreciation for their operating costs. They can thus lose money for quite a long time before it becomes so serious a problem that they can no longer fail to take notice of it and appreciate it for what it is. (In fact, this problem is not confined to small businesses: It happens perhaps even more often in large corporations.)

One of the business cliches we hear often is that "no one ever went broke taking a profit." That sounds like a reasonable statement, and it was probably a reliable general truth once, in a simpler time, when taxes were a relatively minor item of cost and business overhead was typically quite modest. The problem with it is that the meaning of the word *profit* is elusive today, unless it has an adjective to qualify it, such as *gross, pre-tax* or *net*. Unfortunately, also, it is still generally taken to mean that you sold something for more than it cost you, but all too often the small business owner does not know what the true costs are. It is taken to mean that if you paid $3 for an item, you are getting a profit when you sell it for $5. But you may not be taking a profit, not a net profit at least. The *direct* cost may have been $3, but the *indirect* cost may well have added another $3 to the *total* cost, and so you lose money when you sell it for $5, despite the apparent (and deceptive) *gross* profit of $2.

Without knowing—knowing absolutely—what all your costs are, you cannot know whether you are getting a net (e.g., true and final) profit, breaking even or losing money. You cannot know any of these things without an adequate accounting system. In short, then, you cannot know what rates you must get unless you know all your costs associated directly and indirectly with whatever you sell.

That is probably one-half the problem of setting and getting rates that enable you to pay your bills and draw a reasonable salary. It's the guide to setting rates—*minimal* acceptable rates. Eventually we will talk about *getting* the rates you have set—getting your customers to pay them—and we shall talk about getting *top* rates, the rates your superior service deserves to earn. But first problems first. Let's talk first about how you can get a true understanding of "how you are doing"—the financial bottom line of your business venture, so that you can begin to appreciate what rates you must get as the absolute minimum.

To gain that understanding, you must get a clear, unbiased and hardheaded look at the real costs of doing business.

Understanding Costs

In these times of multiple and complex tax structures, it is understandable that so few of us starting in business for the first time understand the cost of being in business, any business. Consider, for example, these as the inescapable minimal cost categories of any venture launched and conducted responsibly:

- Rent/mortgage payments
- Heat, light, other utilities
- Telephone, voice and fax
- Insurance, all kinds
- Taxes, all kinds
- Equipment
- Supplies
- Advertising
- Miscellaneous

Classifying and Labeling Costs

Costs show up (are listed and entered into the records) in many forms, especially in the complex accounting systems of large corporations, and they are classified, defined and/or labeled in various ways, according to the analysis you are trying to make and the understanding you want to reach. (More on this in a moment.)

Even a small business may have a ledger sheet that lists 20 or more kinds of ongoing, daily costs. They include the items just listed, but in greater detail. In my own case, my rent payment includes payment for light, heat, water, repairs and trash removal, so these costs do not show up on my books as separate items. But I do have such miscellaneous items as postage stamps, advertising, dues, subscriptions, travel, marketing and office supplies; I do have minor and major equipment expenses, as well as taxes and other costs. Some of my costs are fixed—rent and insurance, for example—while others are variable: Postage, printing and telephone are usually variable costs. Then there are occasional or one-time costs, such as repairs and major equipment purchases.

Costs are defined and classified in more than one way, and any cost item may appear under more than one category, according to the system you use, the analysis you are making or the understanding you are trying to reach. *Fixed* and *variable* represent one way to consider costs. On the other hand, it is more significant in many ways to recognize and lump together two other broad categories of costs: Direct and indirect. Each set of definitions has its own uses, depending on what you want to know about the financial or economic side of your business.

One goal that makes it more significant to differentiate between direct and indirect costs is that of trying to get a basic understanding of profit and loss in a way that defines the minimal rates you can charge for your service. Direct and indirect costing tells you what your total or absolute cost is so that you can easily calculate the minimum price you can charge without losing money—really losing money, that is. Thus, it is essential that you understand this most basic distinction, explained in the following paragraphs.

Direct Costs

In most service businesses, the principal direct cost is the cost of labor applied to a customer's project—billable labor, that is. That is true whether it is your labor or that of employees. If you pay yourself or an employee $40 an hour and the project requires 400 hours of that labor, it imposes a direct cost of $16,000. You must actually pay out that amount of money to get the job done. However, that is only the part of the cost that you paid one or more individuals.

You may have other direct costs. If you had to undertake travel as part of the project, those costs are direct costs. If you had to print a report as part of the project, that is a direct cost. Any cost that is incurred strictly and entirely for a given customer and project is a direct cost. It is directly identified with and incurred directly for a given project. It is a cost incurred only because that project exists, and it would otherwise never have been incurred.

Indirect Costs

Direct costs are never the only costs of doing a job for a customer. There are those taxes, insurance, rent, office supplies, depreciation and many other costs mentioned here earlier. They are imposed on you even before you can apply that $16,000 worth of direct labor, and you would experience most of these costs whether you had done that project or not.

Let us assume, for convenience, that labor is the only direct cost (you have no travel, printing or other direct costs for this example). Let us assume also, to make this example clear, that you had no other projects. You experience perhaps another $8,000 worth of cost for those office supplies, telephone charges, equipment, marketing and supplies. It thus costs you a total of $24,000 to provide the service, or $60 an hour. Charging the customer anything less than $60 an hour involves an immediate true loss. Charging $60 an hour is "trading dollars." You are not taking a profit but only recovering your costs, while you are also assuming a normal business risk and are thus always close to losing money. (You are always on the edge of loss, if you are working without profit because you then have no margin for even a slight error.) Thus, $60 per hour is the minimum you can charge without ensuring that you will lose money, and even that does not ensure that you will not lose money. Your price is based on your estimate of what it will take to do the job—400 hours at $40 per hour—but since it is only an estimate, you are still running some risk of losing money through underestimate or any chance circumstance that might require more time and effort than you anticipated. Without a profit percentage, you are not covered for that risk, as you are entitled to be. That, compensating for the risk, is one of the reasons a profit is not only justified but necessary.

There is a common name applied to these indirect costs every business encounters and must pay. It is called *overhead*. And yet, as is the case with other terms introduced here, overhead does not have a single definition but varies in its meaning according to how it is used in the accounting system employed.

Overhead

Of course, you do not normally rent your office for a given customer and job, nor do you buy insurance, advertising and office supplies on the basis of a single project. (There are exceptions to this, but they are not relevant to this discussion.)

There is thus no way that you can prorate or determine absolutely how much of your insurance, marketing expense and telephone bill ought to be charged against any given customer and job. Yet, those costs must be recovered, if you are to pay your bills and stay in business. Finding a method for doing that gives rise to that familiar term, "overhead," that many of us use freely and understand in principle, perhaps, but do not understand fully.

Overhead is the cost of keeping your doors open. To a large extent, it is fixed. Your rent is the same, whether you do a lot of or a little bit of business. Your insurance is probably the same, as are many other indirect costs. On the other hand, some costs vary with the amount of business you do. When you are busy, you probably have higher telephone costs, use more postage, use up office supplies faster and have larger tax bills.

To recover those kinds of costs in your prices, you must find a method to prorate those costs so that a fair percentage is represented in your billing rates. To do that, we normally establish an *overhead rate.*

It probably should be noted here that establishing a single overhead rate as a percentage of direct labor dollars is a general practice for service businesses in which material is not a significant cost factor—i.e., is a small fraction of the cost—and so is usually not charged directly to the customer. Those businesses in which material is a major item of cost and is billed directly to the customer and project—a home remodeling business, for example—often have a second overhead figure applied to materials, reflecting the administrative and other costs of buying, storing and supplying materials. Too many businesses include a "G&A" or general and administrative cost figure as another class of indirect costs, but that is usually a practice of relatively large organizations. Here, we will assume that we are dealing entirely with service businesses applying a single overhead rate as a percentage of direct labor costs.

The Overhead Rate

Rate is a proportion or percentage, rather than an absolute figure. If you had only one customer and project for the whole year, you could project your overhead or indirect cost as an absolute figure. In the example used earlier, where your direct cost was $16,000 (400 hours and $40 per hour) and your total indirect cost was $8,000, that represented a rate of 50 percent: $8,000/$16,000 = 50%. (Indirect cost divided by direct cost = overhead rate.)

A 50-percent overhead rate thus means that you add 50 cents to every dollar of direct labor to ascertain and recover your total cost. So if you pay out $40 an hour to yourself or another employee, you must rate the work as costing you $60 an hour. Your hourly billing rate must thus reflect that $60 plus some profit figure— perhaps 10 to 20 percent additional—i.e., $66 to $72 per hour.

Of course, business is usually not that simple, and overhead rates are not such even, easy-to-work-with numbers. Nor can you arbitrarily set your hourly rate wherever you want it. Perhaps in your field or your set of circumstances $66 an hour is a high rate and not easy to command. Perhaps it is difficult to command more than $45 an hour. There are various reasons for such wide variations. One individual, a highly trained graduate of MIT in information sciences, recently established himself as an independent consultant and appealed to a group of his fellow computer consultants for guidance in setting his rates. The response was a mixed one.

One respondent advised that new consultant to decide what his skills and specialties justified as an annual salary and earn that by charging customers a daily rate of 1 percent of that figure or, as an example, $1,000 per day if he considered himself to be a

$100,000 per year consultant. That, according to this adviser, was a simple formula that should provide for typical expenses and produce the desired salary.

Another respondent pointed out that location makes a big difference. For example, she pointed out, in Portland, Oregon, rates average on the order of $45 to $60 per hour, while in Los Angeles, California, they tend more to $75 to $100 per hour.

Bear in mind that these and other formulas or standards offered by others are individual opinions and reflect individual experiences. They may or may not represent sound operating principles for you. But they are guidelines, of a sort, and they do serve to make you aware that there are many different factors involved in setting and getting the right rates for your work. In the end, despite all well-intentioned advice, you must base your decisions on your own experience and circumstances.

Let's take a quick look at what the formula of charging 1 percent of one's annual salary as a daily rate is likely to produce in practice.

Nominally, there are 260 business or working days in the year. Assuming that you take the normal days off each year for vacation, holidays, illness and special occasions, probably on the order of 25 days per year, that leaves you with 235 days of work. There is scant chance that you will work five days or 40 hours of each working week of the year. You will have to devote some time to administrative chores and marketing. It is reasonable to allow at least 25 percent of your working time for that, bringing your billable days down to about 176 days. That, according to the formula offered, will produce $176,000 in billing. To earn a $1,000-a-day rate, you must therefore operate at an overhead rate of less than 76 percent, if you are to cover all expenses and be able to bank a profit.

That may work out, if you can manage to keep your overhead down. That is, you can take about 15 percent profit if you can keep your overhead to not more than 53 percent. (The numbers are rounded off, for convenience, but they are quite close to the precise figures the formula and stated premises would produce.)

That illustrates briefly how important your overhead rate can be. Let's discuss that in the next chapter.

Chapter 5

Establishing Your Overhead Rate

It is easy enough to calculate a proper overhead rate, once the overhead is defined. That isn't always as simple as it may seem. Because overhead is not necessarily a precise term, it can mean what you want it to mean or what your business conditions dictate.

Overhead versus Indirect Costs Generally

It is easy enough to define overhead in general terms as the indirect costs of doing business, to establish an overhead rate, and to break overhead costs down into the individual expense items that constitute overhead—what *you* define as overhead, that is. You can define it to suit your own ideas of what constitutes the best accounting practices for your needs. In fact, different organizations do use the term somewhat differently. To be more precise, they differ in what they include as items of overhead and in what they prefer to identify as other kinds of items of indirect cost that belong to quite another expense pool. In fact, while overhead may be broadly defined as the indirect costs of doing business and is generally regarded as being all but synonymous with indirect costs, not all indirect costs are necessarily overhead, and not all overhead costs are necessarily indirect but may be simply assigned to overhead arbitrarily as a convenience. So you do have a certain amount of flexibility in dealing with overhead.

That flexibility is what makes overhead a somewhat arbitrary term. For some, overhead and indirect costs are synonymous, and overhead then includes every cost that is not charged directly to the individual customer. For others, overhead is only one category of indirect cost, and there are others, or at least one other.

Before exploring this, bear in mind that none of this changes the basic truth: You must recover *all* costs, regardless of what they are called or where and how they appear in your records. Categorizing and classifying costs is done for the purpose of control and management—to make each cost visible for those purposes. Thus, they may appear in different cost groups and under different titles or classifications, but they must all be included, finally, in the figure you quote a customer as the price of whatever the customer wants and you promise to deliver. This will become more evident when we look at some typical cost projections you may have to make in pursuing projects. Figure 5.1, a summary cost analysis, illustrates the basic relationships between direct and indirect costs.

This is a summary presentation, not at all complete, and is intended here only to show you the application of indirect costs to the total bill and the importance of doing this accurately because it does affect the final price quite substantially.

Figure 5.1 **Summary of Direct and Indirect Costs**

Direct Costs

Direct Labor: Writing: 4 hours @ $44/hour $156
              Illustrating: 2 hours @ $30/hour 60
              Typing and Proofing: 1 hour @ $28/hour 28
              Total Direct Labor 244

Overhead: $244 @ 0.68 166
Other Direct Costs: Printing and Copying 22

              Total Direct Costs and Overhead $432

Note here the overhead rate applies to the direct labor dollars but not to the other direct costs, such as printing, that are posted after the total labor costs, direct and indirect, are calculated and posted in the cost analysis. This is because the major portion of overhead costs are incurred in connection with labor. Insurance, taxes and fringe benefits are also among the major overhead items, especially in a labor-intensive operation, such as a service business.

It is possible to create a separate overhead cost to cover the indirect cost of acquiring, storing and providing materials where those are major elements of a business, and we shall cover that a bit later in this chapter. For a great many service businesses, it hardly pays to do the additional bookkeeping when other direct costs, such as materials and subcontracting or purchased support services, are trivial portions of the whole cost. In such cases, it is the common practice to add these minor direct costs to the general overhead expense pool and recover them in that way or via another kind of indirect expense pool, often designated general and administrative expenses. We shall come to that also a bit later. On the other hand, there are some classes of other direct costs, such as consulting, subcontracting and other support costs that are significant elements of the total cost, and you ought to apply some indirect costs to them. You will see some examples of this later.

The chief distinction normally made by those who choose to break indirect costs down into classes, of which overhead is only one (although usually the principal one), is between overhead and fringe benefits. Perhaps there is some psychological/marketing advantage to breaking out and identifying this one class of indirect costs. One advantage may be a psychological one, in that it reduces the nominal overhead rate, since fringe benefits then acquire a separate rate. That may make the cost package a bit more palatable in those jobs where you may be required to reveal your overhead rate. (Large government contracts usually require such disclosure, for example, and many government contracting officers tend to regard high overhead rates with great suspicion as signs of inefficiency that is costly to the government.) I have never perceived an advantage for my own purposes in having a separate cost pool for fringe benefits, but it is an option you may wish to consider, if you believe it will help you in some manner. (The matter of presenting costs in a way that makes them most palatable is a subject that is an important element of marketing.) I think it simpler and just as useful, in most cases, to place all indirect costs into a common expense pool identified as overhead. I happen to think that there is a psychological advantage of another kind—how this approach beneficially influences your own thinking—in an overhead rate that includes all indirect costs, making you highly conscious of indirect costs and stimulating you to examine them closely and with reduction in mind. On the other hand, I can see that the alternate practice may serve the same purpose by highlighting that portion of indirect costs (fringe benefits, that is). It may make one more conscious of where the money goes and what makes the cost of doing business so high today.

Fringe Benefits

The costs identified as fringe benefits are all costs incurred to provide benefits directly to employees, over and above their salaries. (Continue to bear in mind, as pointed out earlier you are or ought to consider yourself to be an employee of your business, whether you are a sole proprietor, a partner or a corporation, and whether you have other employees or not. If you are a corporation, however, you have greater latitude in bestowing fringe benefits on yourself and being able to charge them off as business expenses.) They may be benefits you bestow voluntarily on yourself and other employees, or they may be benefits the law requires you to provide. Accordingly, the following are among the principal items that would normally be included in an expense pool identified as fringe benefits:

- Paid time off from work:
  - Vacation or personal leave time
  - Sick leave
  - Maternity leave

- Military-duty leave
- Holidays
- Company-paid insurance:
  - Life insurance
  - Medical/hospitalization insurance
- Other:
  - Bonuses
  - Company picnics/other such events

Of course, you may not include all these in your plan, and you may have other items that do not appear here. You may have, also, unpaid maternity leave or leave for military duty, so although they could be properly considered fringe benefits, they would not be part of your expense pool.

The costs of fringe benefits would tend to be rather stable, if not fixed, unless you were doing a great deal of hiring and terminating employees. If you separate them from other overhead items, you will want to present them somewhat differently, as in Figure 5.2. In the figure, it is assumed that fringe benefits represent 20 percent of direct labor dollars. The net result is the same final cost, however, as it should be.

Figure 5.2   Cost Calculation of Fringe Benefits

Direct Costs

Direct Labor: Writing: 4 hours @ $44/hour $156
                            Illustrating: 2 hours @ $30/hour   60
                            Typing and Proofing: 1 hr @ $28/hour   28
                            Total Direct Labor   244

Overhead: $244 @ 0.48   117

Fringe benefits: $244 @ 0.20   49

Other Direct Costs: Printing and Copying   22

                            Total Direct Costs and Overhead $432

General and Administrative (G&A) Costs

Many organizations, especially large ones with more than one office or division, have still another kind of indirect expense, referred to generally as "G&A" that represents a class of indirect costs titled General and Administrative costs, which I referred to briefly a few paragraphs ago. This is a rather special kind of indirect expense and is intended to identify and explain certain special kinds of expenses that might be troublesome to recover otherwise. Let's take the case of the organization with several offices, for example.

The organization with several offices necessarily has a headquarters office that may even be physically separate from all operating divisions of the company. Headquarters, wherever it is located, houses employees who do work that does not produce income directly—e.g., the corporate comptroller, the executive vice-president and the purchasing agent do not carry out the specific functions that the customers pay for, so they definitely represent indirect costs. Yet, they do not directly supervise or support the income-producing workers of the operating divisions either, nor are they even part of any income-producing units. Thus, they are not really part of overhead, the indirect cost of supporting those whose work produces the organization's income. (Admittedly, the distinctions become blurred a bit here, but many organizations find it desirable, if not necessary, to make these distinctions.) That makes it difficult to justify charging their work as overhead. It is indirect cost, it must be recovered, and yet there is a problem assigning it to the overhead expense pool.

To cover this kind of indirect expense, many organizations use the G&A charge, a fixed rate that every operating branch or division must add to their prices. In the situation of a corporation with many offices, I have always perceived G&A as a kind of tax on each of the offices to pay for the corporate headquarter's support function. Where overhead must cover all the expenses of supporting the workers whose functions produce income, G&A must cover all the expenses of supporting the offices with corporate services, such as doing the payroll and providing national advertising. The assignment of G&A costs is shown in Figure 5.3.

Figure 5.3   Adding G&A Costs to the Cost Calculation

```
Direct Costs

Direct Labor:  Writing: 4 hours @ $44/hour ................................. $156
               Illustrating: 2 hours @ $30/hour .............................  60
               Typing and Proofing: 1 hour @ $28/hour ................  28
                      Total Direct Labor .........................................  244

Overhead: $244 @ 0.48 ...............................................................  117

Fringe benefits: $244 @ 0.20 .......................................................  49

Other Direct Costs: Printing and Copying ....................................  22

                      Total Direct Costs and Overhead ............. $432

G&A Costs @ 0.065 ..................................................................  28

                      Subtotal ........................................... $460
```

Note that G&A is added after the overhead figure, so that everything above it—direct labor, overhead and other direct costs—is covered.

There are some other kinds of indirect costs that are normally covered by G&A, but in general they are costs that do not fit the categories of overhead or fringe benefits. The one-office business is not likely to have need for a G&A expense pool (although there are exceptions to this), but it is helpful to understand what G&A is, even if it does not affect you and your own business. A bit later we will look at how G&A is fitted into price estimates and how it affects the final price or bottom line. (If subcontracting or other support is a factor, it would appear before the G&A total so that the contractor would bill the client for that cost also.)

G&A costs also tend to be rather stable or virtually fixed, changing infrequently. Too, it is usually a relatively small percentage figure when compared with overhead costs.

Overhead

That leaves overhead as the expense pool for all remaining indirect costs of heat, light, advertising, printing, marketing, delivery, repairs, depreciation, postage, shipping, supplies, subscriptions and others. In practice, you would probably not have such general cost terms as "marketing," but you would cover that kind of expense in greater detail as "entertainment," "travel," "automobile rental," "advertising," "memberships," "exhibits" and other specific marketing expenses. You would decide whether an individual item, such as "subscriptions," was a big enough item of expense to justify breaking it down into specific details, as marketing usually is. (Note that some of these kinds of expenses may appear also in a G&A expense pool, although they would necessarily have to be identified as separate and distinct from those charged as overhead.)

Controlling Influences

As long as you are a sole proprietor you have a great deal of latitude in how you organize your accounts and where you list various costs. If you are incorporated, you have a few restrictions imposed by your state's laws, especially if you are a public corporation with stockholders. And if you are a government contractor, you have some restrictions imposed by the requirements of government regulations affecting procurement with public money in those procurements where you are required to disclose your accounting method and meet government standards. This requirement is sometimes a problem for a contractor pursuing a government contract for the first time and trying to meet the requirements of the request for proposal. This requirement is also a reason often given for the introduction of G&A as a class of indirect costs resulting from government objections to certain items of cost included as part of the overhead. Some government contracting officials would accept most indirect costs as overhead items but would balk at certain others, such as costs of a remote corporate management office, insisting that these were not properly overhead costs but were general and administrative costs and could be accepted only as such.

The difference between where and how overhead is entered into the cost projections and where and how general and administrative costs are calculated has a marked effect on the bottom line: What the customer must pay. That should be quite evident from even a cursory examination of Figure 5.3. That is, if G&A costs were to be entered above the line "Overhead," they would be subject to the same 48 percent rate and would then show up as $41.44, rather than $28. G&A is another indirect cost, as is overhead, and thus must be a separate item and not itself subject to overhead costs.

There is still another variable about overhead, a variable about the basis for setting the overhead rate. Preferably, overhead ought to be what is referred to as "historical overhead," but circumstances often dictate that a "provisional overhead" rate be used.

Historical versus Provisional Overhead

First, bear clearly in mind that overhead is a figure, a number of dollars spent to support those functions for which the customer is charged directly. That is principally labor in the case of most service businesses. Overhead rate is the ratio of those indirect costs to direct labor costs. Generally speaking, the overhead rate is calculated thus for businesses in which almost all the direct cost is labor:

$$\text{Indirect costs} \div \text{Direct labor costs} \times 100 = \text{Overhead rate}$$
$$\text{Example: } 600 \div 100 \times 100 = 60\%$$

If your business happens to be such that materials are a major part of what you deliver to your customers, you may very well wish to have a separate overhead for materials, for it does cost money to buy, stock and dispense materials to customers. The principle of a materials overhead is the same as the above, substituting material cost for direct labor cost and substituting the indirect cost of supplying materials as the materials overhead cost.

You will have to keep a record of the indirect costs associated with the materials and including all costs to you. The total cost of materials you sell to customers or charge as part of whatever it is that you provide customers is more than the simple acquisition costs of the materials. Your total costs include such items as these:

- Administrative time devoted to selecting and buying the materials
- Cost of the associated paperwork
- Storage (inventory) cost
- Shrinkage (spoilage, etc.) of materials
- Packing and shipping

You are entitled to take some profit in your markup of materials, and that should be added to the price you charge your customers for the materials. (Presumably, if materials are a major item delivered to customers, they are identified and billed in your invoices.)

In estimating a job where you are billing materials and material overhead, therefore, you calculate the cost to you of the materials needed and then mark that figure up by your materials overhead and your profit margin, as shown in Figure 5.4.

Figure 5.4 **Adding Materials Overhead to the Cost Calculation**

Direct Costs	
Direct Labor: Writing: 4 hours @ $44/hour	$156
Illustrating: 2 hours @ $30/hour	60
Typing and Proofing: 1 hour @ $28/hour	28
Total Direct Labor	244
Labor Overhead: $244 @ 0.48	117
Fringe Benefits: $244 @ 0.20	49
Other Direct Costs: Materials	22
Materials Overhead at 18%	4
Total Direct Costs and Overhead	$436
G&A Costs @ 0.065	28
Subtotal	$464

You can handle subcontracted and vended work, such as printing, delivery, copying, computer programming, consultant services, temporary or casual labor, or other contract functions in a similar manner. You are entitled to calculate the support costs of such work and use both an overhead and a fee or profit margin in arriving at a final price.

This much in calculating an overhead rate is easy enough to understand and do, as the simple examples show. A problem often arises when you try to get an accurate tally of your overhead dollars and your direct labor dollars; you need both to determine your overhead rate with any accuracy.

Having kept accurate records, you know what these figures are for last year, and you normally use these as the basis for estimating costs for your current projects. You normally assume, of course, that last year's figures are still typical—that there has been no serious change in the totals of either your overhead or your direct labor. That is known generally as "historical overhead" for the obvious reason that it is based on the history represented by your books.

You set overhead rates on the assumption that there has been no significant change, but there has been some change, even if it is not a great change: Business is dynamic, not static. It *does* change to some extent, at least. Thus, your overhead is inevitably an estimate based on that assumption and is thus rarely completely accurate, but it has some margin of error.

The situation is even worse the first year you are in business because you have no history as yet; your overhead rate is based entirely on your best estimates of how much direct labor you will bill and how much indirect cost you will have. That is often referred to as "provisional overhead." It is accurate, *provided* that your estimates prove accurate. But even after you have been in business for a few years, you may call your overhead rate historical, but it is still provisional to the extent that your assumptions of typical costs and ratios prove true. So "historical overhead" is an assumption, a necessary convenience. (In major government contacts, it is not unusual for the government to require an audit at the end of the contract to verify the validity of the overhead charged and to make adjustments, if necessary.)

How Direct Labor Can Affect the Overhead Rate

Overhead includes both fixed and variable costs, although much of your overhead is fixed. Your rent or mortgage payments are fixed, for example; some of your advertising costs are contracted for and are fixed for at least the duration of that contract (Yellow Pages advertising, for example); installment payments on fixtures, furniture or equipment are usually fixed, and even variable costs are often variable to only a limited extent. As a result, the volume of direct labor is often the chief cause of variable overhead. That is, your overhead rate is dependent on direct labor figures, since it is a ratio that can be changed by a variation in either of the costs constituting the ratio.

That may come as a surprise, but consider the following hypothetical scenario as a typical case:

For example, let us suppose that $25,000 in annual overhead costs breaks down along the following lines:

Fixed costs	$12,000
Semi-fixed costs	3,000
Variable costs	10,000
Total overhead costs	$25,000

Let us further postulate that your historic direct labor total has been $40,000. That works out to 25,000/40,000 = 0.625 or 62.5 percent overhead rate.

Now let us suppose that you have had a slow year, and your direct labor total has declined to $30,000. That ought to affect your overhead costs along the following line:

Fixed costs	$12,000
Semi-fixed costs	2,000
Variable costs	7,500
Total overhead costs	$21,500

Now your overhead is 21,500/30,000 = 0.7166 or 71.67 percent. Thus, if you calculate your costs this year based on a 62.5

percent overhead, you will lose money. (In my own case, my direct labor figure has varied as much as 50 percent from best-year to worst-year.)

Of course, it works the other way too. If you were to increase your direct labor by as much as 50 percent, with direct labor going to $60,000, the effect is equally dramatic:

> Fixed costs $15,000
> Semi-fixed costs 4,500
> Variable costs 13,500
> Total overhead costs $33,000

Now the calculation is 33,000/60,000 = 0.55 or 55 percent. It is a reason for bidding on a large contract at a lower than usual unit rate because it will drive your overhead down and give you enough increase in markup to enable you to work at the lower unit rate without compromise to profitability overall. Some firms take on large projects with the justifying rationalization that the large project provides cash flow and "pays the rent," but the truth is that a project that is large enough to result in a material increase in direct labor also drives down the overhead rate and thus increases markup.

What Is "Markup"?

"Markup" is a term more often found in retailing proprietary products than in service enterprises, but the concept is applicable to both kinds of businesses. In the retail business, the term refers to the difference between what the retailer pays for merchandise and what he or she sells it for.

The ratio of cost to selling price varies widely among various types of merchandise. If a television receiver manufacturer sets its recommended retail price at $300 but discounts it 40 percent to dealers (sells it to dealers at $180), the manufacturer is recommending a 66 percent markup ($180 × 0.666 = $120 markup). In fact, few major appliances today are sold at the full manufacturers' recommended prices, but are discounted and sold at markups of closer to 20 or 25 percent, and perhaps even less in some cases. That would make the $300 TV sell at about $225 ($180 × 0.25 = $45 markup).

Discounting tends to be more feasible for retailers than for service businesses because sales figures in them are not closely bound to labor costs as they are in service businesses. Most service businesses are labor-intensive by their very nature—i.e., essentially, labor is what you sell in a service business. Therefore, labor costs increase significantly in a service business when sales increase.

That relationship between labor costs and labor rates is reversed in a service business. In a service business, as direct labor costs rise in proportion to sales volume, the overhead rate necessarily declines, while overhead costs rise only to a much lesser degree. It is thus very much to your advantage to survey your accounts frequently, especially when there has been some change in your sales volume, to see what your true overhead is and adjust your prices accordingly. Unless your sales/work volume is reasonably constant, your overhead rate can vary quite a lot. Of course, you do not want to change your estimated overhead rate and thus your billing rates every month, so you try to determine what your average overhead rate is for the year, and you use that as the basis for estimating. Still, there are exceptional cases. For the service business that is based on winning projects via competitive bidding, the workload and therefore the direct labor volume can vary widely. That is a major reason such companies tend to use contract temporaries, rather than recruit and terminate employees frequently. You will normally pay a temporary a higher hourly rate than you would pay a direct employee, but there are fewer fringe benefits and virtually no associated recruitment and termination costs. If you are pursuing a major project that will greatly increase the amount of direct labor you will have to apply, you should take into account in estimating the job the effect the contract will have on your overhead rate, should you win it. That can make a major difference in your costs and may very well make it feasible to undertake a major project at considerably less than your normal rates because your overhead will be driven down and your markup will therefore go up. Let's consider this in a hypothetical example.

Let us suppose that your typical annual direct labor amounts to $80,000 and your historical overhead rate is 65 percent, or $52,000. You expect that to continue. However, you suddenly have an unexpected opportunity to compete for a project that you anticipate will call for doubling your direct labor for the year. At your typical overhead rate, you would have an additional $132,000 (plus your profit markup). However, you believe that you must be highly competitive to win this new project, so you calculate the real added cost of taking it on.

The chances are that you will add about one-third of the direct-labor cost to your overhead, even if you recruit permanent employees, represented principally by increases in taxes, fringe benefits and insurance. That would mean that if you won the project, while maintaining your normal workload, your total overhead cost would rise to about $78,640, but your overhead rate—as a ratio with the $160,000 direct labor total—would drop to about 49 percent (78,640 divided by 160,000, multiplied by 100, or 49 percent). You could thus afford to bid this job at $119,200. (You might do considerably better by using temporaries, and I would advise always calculating this as an alternative that may enable you to be even more competitive in your pricing, while still affording you a boon in greater-than-average profits.)

Actually, there is an additional benefit to be had: You would experience some additional profit from the projects you already have under contract, which you brought in at a 65 percent overhead because you would be performing at least part of them at a lower overhead, which would then become profit.

Some companies handle this kind of situation a bit differently. Instead of calculating the reduced overhead rate that would result from winning the new project, they bid at what they call break-even—i.e., with zero fee or profit included in the estimate and quoted price. Actually, they do earn profits because the new project shoulders some of the existing overhead. In defense contracting, executives often referred to "supporting the overhead" as the justification or need for undertaking any contract at a nominal or nonexistent fee. The implication of the term was that when business was slow and new contracts difficult to get, it was wise to take on any contract "to meet the payroll" (another favorite expression for breakeven contracting). Or, where a contractor has customarily enjoyed cost-plus contracts, he may be concerned with keeping his overhead at a high rate because his contract guarantees reimbursement of that high overhead expense!

Special Situations

These discussions have been based on the two extreme situations, one in which direct costs other than labor are so small as to be insignificant, and the other case in which materials, subcontracts, purchased support services and other direct costs (other than labor, that is) are a significant part of what must be billed to the customer. In those cases, the decision is clear-cut. However, between those extremes lie a great many cases in which the situation is far less clear-cut because the dollar amount of those costs is not great and the decision is necessarily an arbitrary one. Here, to make the issue clear, are a few of those types of costs commonly encountered and often arbitrarily assigned:

▪ Consulting	▪ Temporary labor	▪ Telephone charges
▪ Travel	▪ Printing/copying	▪ Laboratory work
▪ Postage	▪ Delivery/shipping	▪ Supplies/materials
▪ Telephone	▪ Faxes	▪ Storage

Note that this is not a matter of whether you would or would not charge these costs to the customer. They are expenses, and you must recover them. The uncertainty is whether to recover these costs as other direct costs or as overhead costs. The pros and cons are these:

As costs to be charged as other direct costs, along with associated indirect costs, this imposes a burden of recordkeeping, even of each long-distance telephone call or fax, of postage expenditures and of other items that might be considered to be "incidental" costs. It adds also to the burden of accounting in general and of invoicing accounts. It can be a time-consuming daily chore, as well as an additional bookkeeping expense. It does, however, help keep control over your overhead rate.

On the other hand, if you simply charge these off as incidentals, to be charged to the overhead expense pool, you need not make individual records of these costs, but you do increase your overhead costs and rate by the sum of such small occasional expenses. That is an unfair burdening of your overhead, charging to it costs that are really direct and not indirect costs. It hurts your business, in the end, by burdening your overhead. Unless these items are truly incidental and minor, it is usually worth the trouble to make and keep careful records and bill them as part of the direct costs.

Chapter 6

Building Overhead into Your Billings

Overhead is not a fiction; overhead dollars are as real as are all other dollars you must spend to conduct your business. You recover them in your billings, or you don't recover them at all.

It's Really Simple Arithmetic

An important point that has been made earlier both expressly and by firm implication (in the previous chapter, for example) is worth repeating here as a reminder and preamble to what must be said in this chapter: In business, if you are even to survive, let alone prosper, all your costs must be recovered in one way or another as some part of the income of the business. Usually, that recovery of all costs is built into your normal selling prices—your rates and project estimates. That is, your billing rates must include all costs, direct and indirect. Thus, your costs inevitably *dictate* your billing rates.

There are exceptions here, as in all things. One exception is the case in which you are willing to subsidize your business—lose money deliberately—as a marketing device, i.e., to offer prospects "loss leaders" to gain new customers. The loss leader is a more or less standard (at least widely used and time-honored) marketing gambit used in all kinds of businesses to stimulate sales. The philosophy is to attract new customers with the expectation that you can also do additional profitable transactions with them. Retailers may refer to this goal as creating more traffic in their places of business.

Another exception is the case where you offer rebates, for which the customer must apply after the sale. It has become another popular marketing device, with marketers using the gambit to announce bargain prices, followed by a small-print amendment that says "after rebate." Fortunately, relatively few customers actually do apply for the rebates, or the plan would not be a sound— profitable—sales inducement. Thus, while you might lose money on some of your sales, most of them would be profitable because you would not have to rebate anything to the majority of customers.

Still another exception is the case where the product is inexpensive to produce and the vendor requires a substantial "shipping and handling" cost in addition to the bargain price. That defrays the expense and furnishes a small profit. In fact, some vendors have advertised "free" items, asking only for the shipping and handling charge.

These are all marketing strategies, and if some resulting sales are made at less than the cost, the difference is charged off as marketing expense, itself an overhead item, to be recovered in the billing prices for other items. In that sense, it is still not a loss and is still to be recovered as part of overhead costs. So, despite marketing strategies and rationales of various kinds, the basic principle is still a firm one: You must recover all costs. Overhead is not, of course, the only cost. But there are two reasons for addressing a special chapter to its recovery. One is that for many kinds of business, overhead is by far the greatest cost of doing business. The other is that overhead is a cost that is too often allowed to creep up until it is far too great. Thus, overhead requires great vigilance to prevent its creep upward. Being highly conscious of its influence in setting your prices should help you maintain a great awareness of the necessity for its control.

There are occasionally other exceptional circumstances than those mentioned here, such as certain kinds of contracts in which the customer underwrites the vendor's overhead as a separate item. However, let us here consider the normal commercial situations. Most typical, probably, is the one in which you expect to operate your business at a profit without tricky marketing strategies—sales "gimmicks" of any kind, that is. The other is one in which you have committed yourself to a fixed price or maximum number of hours and underestimated your costs for a given job or the number of hours required to get it done. That does not necessarily mean you must lose money on the job, however, if you have been wise in contracting for it. But that, protecting yourself against the uncertainties of estimating the requirements of custom projects, is a subject properly addressed later as part of discussions in Chapters 8 and 9.

The Cost of Nonbillable Time

Your objective in a service business is to maximize your billable time, time for which customers are billed, because all nonbillable time is overhead cost. However, it is not possible to have 100-percent billable time for more than one reason when you are the proprietor. It is inescapable that you will spend some portions of your time in nonbillable, overhead activities. If you are the typical small business owner, probably one-third or more of your time is not billable to anyone but yourself and is probably spent mostly in marketing activities.

However, you will also be spending part of that time in necessary administrative and miscellaneous chores that are also necessary to conduct your business. You can't avoid that necessity, even if you use public accountants and other such services to relieve yourself of personally posting your books and billing your accounts. Be prepared for that, and while you should try to avoid having more than one-third of your time spent in nonbillable activity, you should assume that as the probable portion of your time you must charge to your own overhead.

As a rule, the amount of nonbillable time is not a matter of choice. Most of us give complete priority to billable time, and we will put off doing any other chore until such time as we have no billable work to do. We hope that it will not be long before we are heavily engaged in billable work again, and we tend to give priority of nonbillable time to marketing, in quest of billable time. However, regardless of how and why we have nonbillable time in any quantity, large or small, we must structure our rates to recover the cost. A realistic approach is to allow approximately one-third of your time for nonbillable tasks, such as marketing and administration. You can and should change that one-third to whatever you find necessary, as your experience reveals to you how much of your time you must devote to nonbillable work.

Possibly you will be an exception to the rule and be so in demand that you will have virtually no nonbillable time: You will bill every hour of your normal working day to some faithful customer. You will do all your nonbillable work after business hours, donating them to your company as unpaid time that is not accounted for. Even if you do this as a practical necessity, it would be wise to treat that nearly complete load of billable time as an unusual case. Your donation of great blocks of your spare time would be a questionable and probably unwise policy in terms of maturing your business, and in any case it is not likely to be a permanent state of affairs, but only an occasional condition. (Presumably, if your business has grown so much that you have no nonbillable time—no time to perform marketing and administrative chores—during the normal workweek, you will have hired someone to help you.

Most of us are not that fortunate in having a full load of billable time from the outset and steadily on a long-term basis. But let us suppose that you are so blessed. Examine your circumstances closely: You may find that apparent blessing of superabundance to be not a blessing at all but perhaps the result of your practice of working at some rate well below the market. It is not an unusual case. Unfortunately, when you have built a clientele based on below-market prices, you will probably find it difficult to raise your prices to competitive levels without finding that your customers are suddenly very unhappy to lose their bonanza of cheap labor. They can become quite resentful of your price increases and resist them quite vigorously. It is always easier to start high and lower prices than to do the reverse.

Early success, in this manner, can be a serious problem, and not only because it creates a great difficulty in raising your rates to a more competitive and more profitable level. Early success sometimes misleads a new entrepreneur into the belief that success is easy to achieve, and subsequently leads to careless business practices and policies that lead to disaster. Let us assume, however, that yours is the more typical case, such as most of us find it to be.

Most of us have periods of idle time. We don't think of it as idle time, for we put it to use: To post our accounts, work on a new brochure, call a few old customers in an effort to drum up new business, send out literature to prospects with the hope of creating a few new customers and to otherwise use the time as gainfully as possible. Still, it is nonbillable time—that is, it is billed to ourselves, to our own business—and so it is overhead.

You know what your *direct* costs are, of course—what you pay for the labor and materials needed to get the job done for the customer. Determining what your *indirect* costs are, with relation to any given customer or project, is more difficult. That is why you develop and use an *overhead rate*, as explained. In short, that is what "building overhead into your billings" means. It is also why I enjoined you to keep your overhead trimmed and make it as lean as possible. A high overhead inevitably translates into a high billing rate, along with all the difficulties of selling your services when your billing rates are high. Obviously, a low overhead means that you can bid work competitively, which is a distinct marketing advantage, of course. But a high billing rate can be a double problem: Not only will it make your marketing more difficult—more difficult to close sales—but it will cut into your profit margin at the same time. Overhead is the enemy of both marketing and profit.

What Is a "High" Billing Rate?

"High" and "low" rates in any business are high or low only as customers perceive the rates and what they think the rates ought to be. Where do they get their notions of what rates ought to be? They get those notions in several ways and from several sources of reference.

One notion comes from what they perceive as the market. This is not always—often is not—the true market. The customer reads advertising in the newspapers, in the Yellow Pages and in the direct mail solicitations they receive. Many of the advertisements—"commercial notices," if you wish to be more genteel—are misleading "come-ons," many of them bait-and-switch advertisements, and so they are not reflective of the true market.

Bear in mind always that at best customers usually perceive only the direct costs, if that, and rarely have any appreciation for the costs of rent, heat, insurance, taxes, depreciation and all other costs that are "hidden"—the true overhead—as far as they are concerned. This is the case especially when you deal with the general public, but it also affects how other businesspeople appraise the situation, although as businesspeople they ought to know better. They tend to discount what your time is worth, especially that time you devote to other matters than satisfying their needs.

When a customer balked at my $500 a day consulting rate, some years ago, when that was a fairly representative consulting rate, she could not know how little of that $500 I could put in my pocket and take home to pay my personal expenses. She should have known better because she was herself the head of a small business, but she thought of me as having no overhead because I worked out of an office at home. Therefore, she envisioned me earning $125,000 a year at her expense.

Of course, the actuality of what I could take home was probably one-third or less of that $125,000 because not only did I have to build in the general overhead costs of rent, heat, light, taxes, supplies, equipment maintenance and depreciation, and insurance—I must pay those expenses, even if my office is in my own home—along with all the incidentals. I had to build in also the nonproductive time, the time I must devote to doing necessary things that do not produce income, at least not directly, but are still required to make possible the activities that do produce income. That is, in fact, a major overhead item, perhaps *the* major overhead cost. One point is that it was the customer's perception of what was a high rate, but there is also the important point that nonincome-producing time is also a major overhead cost.

Hourly versus Alternative Rates

There is a distinct tendency of independent service specialists of all kinds to charge by the hour for their services. It does not even occur to many that perhaps a daily rate or a fixed fee—flat price for the job—may be a better alternative for both the specialist and the customer.

True, it is not always a matter of choice. Where the specialist must or agrees to work on the customer's site, as a virtual temporary or contract employee, there is limited choice. In such circumstances, an hourly or daily rate is the only practical approach to billing and is probably the only approach a customer will accept in those circumstances. But even in other cases, where the service provider works in his or her own facility, the majority of independent service specialists tend always to quote an hourly rate. Perhaps they feel more secure with an hourly rate because that implies guaranteed payment for every hour, although that presumption is not always an accurate one. Still, many consciously avoid being forced to commit themselves to a total price. They appear to find estimating a difficult and hazardous undertaking, and they prefer to avoid it if possible by open-ended billing on an hourly basis.

It may seem that hourly billing solves all problems by providing you with a blank check. It does not work that way, of course. The downside of hourly billing is that the customer is always free to terminate your service on the spur of the moment, whereas the customer is normally committed for the entire project when you have a fixed-price contract signed for it.

Either way, hourly billing rate or fixed price for the job, you face the same problem of making sure that your overhead is covered, factored into your job in one way or another. Alternative methods of pricing your services offer the promise of making your cost estimates more palatable to your customers, but that is a subject to be covered in more detail in a later chapter devoted to getting your prices.

A Special, Often-Overlooked Overhead Item

There is a situation that does not get enough attention in discussion of business problems, possibly because it is not a constant, but it is common enough. It is the problem of the problem customer. One cannot be in a business of any kind without eventually encountering Mr. or Mrs. Problem Customer, a prime cause of assorted kinds of angina.

Some customers can easily give an honest business owner an ulcer and often do just that. They are in the minority, fortunately, but it doesn't require a large number of such customers to constitute a serious business problem and run up your overhead costs. Just today I listened to a familiar lament from Myra, an acquaintance who runs a small service business—writing, editing and associated services, such as proofreading and indexing. She was lamenting the customers who "burn" her in a variety of ways. One such is the customer who takes up Myra's time to discuss his (the customer's) problems. After Myra has spent her time and given freely of her knowledge, the customer contracts for services elsewhere, complaining that Myra's rates are too high! But there are also the customers who resist paying, complain constantly, demand more work than they contracted for and take forever to pay the bill, finally. (Many of these are absolute geniuses at finding methods to stall payment longer than anyone would have thought possible.) Some use the leverage of owing money for work already completed to try to renegotiate a lower price, meanwhile using this as an excuse to delay payment further. And some even write bad checks, which they glibly explain away, probably the extreme case of how one may be "burned" by customers.

The kind of prospect that Myra finds objectionable is difficult to deal with under almost any set of circumstances. One of her questions to me was this: If he or she is in your place of business, and you have reached the conclusion that you are talking to a freeloader who will probably never reward you with an order, how do you terminate the time-wasting session gracefully? (After all, your judgment may be faulty, and you don't want to offend someone who may, after all, turn out to be a customer.) Myra believes she must develop some means for terminating such situations without being offensive. I have a different view on this, but we will talk more on this subject in the next chapter when discussing means for cutting overhead costs.

Also a problem, but one a little more easily handled, is the prospect who calls by telephone to pick your brains. Such an individual is also wasting your time. Some specialists take the position that time is the commodity they sell, but that is not strictly true. The service specialist employs knowledge and service to produce results, and it is results that the service specialist sells. Time is the measure of how much those results are worth—what is required to produce those results, the cost to the specialist. Of course, you cannot refuse to answer an occasional question, nor should you. Think of answering a few questions as a sample of what you sell, a sample that helps you demonstrate your skills and knowledge to a prospect and builds some of that credibility necessary to win customers and contracts. But when a prospect wastes your time with endless questions, you must call a halt before you spend more than a minute or two on it.

The general problem of having your time wasted is tantamount to the problem of the merchant who suffers a chronic "inventory shrinkage," resulting, usually, from a combination of pilferage, accidents, mistakes and, in the case of many kinds of foodstuffs and other edibles, spoilage or going overage.

All these things represent losses. The merchant loses inventory they have paid for, Myra is giving away some time that she ought to be able to sell, and both lose money directly when customers do not pay or take much too long to pay. The loss these things represent must be measured in dollars and recognized as an overhead item. It is a cost of doing business, as much as rent, heat, postage and insurance are costs of doing business.

It is not easy to assign a value to this item of overhead. One must estimate—perhaps even *guesstimate*—what such losses represent, but it is important to arrive at some figure, no matter how small—even 2 or 3 percent, although it may well be much higher a figure. Whatever it is in fact, knowing that you have allocated some portion of overhead to cover such losses is beneficial for your peace of mind, if nothing else: The knowledge that your overhead contemplates and compensates for this loss helps you to be philosophical about it.

Chapter 7

Lowering Your Overhead Costs

Overhead is the enemy of profit, even a threat to survival, for many entrepreneurs. Too often, it becomes a threat to the continued existence of a business venture, the major danger against which you must erect a barrier.

Prevention Is the Best Cure

Allowing overhead costs to rise uncontrollably is undoubtedly one of the most common hazards of all businesses, large and small. It was, for example, a major problem of one large defense contractor in Philadelphia at the time I was employed there in a position to understand the problem. Engineering managers were given free access to the general overhead account to use—i.e., charge time and other expenditures to—for marketing purposes. That is, they did not have to apply for and gain corporate approval for such charges.

The rationale for such freedom of access to overhead accounts was to provide the various engineering departments the means to pay for proposal writing and other devices to find new

119

technological defense contracts, the main reasons for the very existence of the organization. The assumption was that engineering managers would use the resource wisely and only for the intended purpose. However, many engineers whose knowledge of and sensitivity to business problems were severely limited were often having difficulty bringing their incumbent projects in within the budgets allowed for them. The overhead account number soon came to represent free money that could be put to dual use: To help them solve their individual project problems and to pursue new business. Or so it appeared to them. It was easy to rationalize their marketing decisions in this manner, and they did so, concealing even from themselves the truth that they were finding or devising ways to make this windfall a convenient means of compensating for and overcoming underestimates and overruns on their projects.

They found several ways to pay for some of the necessary additional (i.e., overrun) project work out of this bonanza of overhead money. For one thing, they tended to find proposal opportunities for which the research would be helpful to their projects and thus represented "free" infusions of resources. Therefore, they often opted to pursue contract opportunities for the wrong reasons—i.e., not because the potential project was right for the firm, but because work on the proposals could also be useful in solving their project budgetary problems. Not surprisingly, that led to futile proposal efforts and expenses that were pure wastes of money. Needless to say, the overhead costs and rate soon soared to new heights, making it ever more difficult to win new contracts, as it forced estimates for future projects ever higher. It placed the company in the straits of difficulty and was undoubtedly a factor leading eventually to the forced sale of the company.

The late master consultant's consultant, Howard Shenson, reported in one of his books (*The Consultant's Guide to Fee-Setting*, Consultant's Library, 1980) the story of a consultant who said that he had had to make four tries to start his consulting business before he was finally successful. He had to learn, he said, three lessons:

1. The lesson of credit (he had granted it too freely)

2. The lesson of marketing (there had not been enough)

3. The lesson of overhead (there had been too much)

Only when he had learned these three lessons and gotten these three functions under firm control did he finally succeed in building a stable and profitable business.

The typical pattern of overhead is for it to rise steadily as the business grows, especially when business is plentiful and profitable. Young, new businesses tend to have lean overhead; older, established businesses tend to have greatly inflated overhead. Management tends to become generous and a bit careless—"fat, dumb and happy," in the jargon—when they are in the pleasant situation of enjoying ample business at good, profitable rates. They become smug, confident that nothing can ever go wrong again. But then, when business hits one of its inevitable troughs, management suddenly discovers that overhead is too high and begins cost-cutting.

That is always difficult. It is much easier to let overhead rise than to force it back, of course. The mistake is waiting until overhead has risen uncontrollably before taking note of it and facing the need to force it back. It is the classic case of prevention versus cure.

The Two Areas of Inflated Overhead Costs

Among the areas and kinds of overhead costs that I am going to address in this chapter are two that ought not to be in the overhead pool at all. One is the cost of many items that are often charged to overhead for convenience but are not truly overhead costs and are therefore unjustified as overhead burdens. The other area, and probably the more serious one, is that of costs that should not have been incurred at all as costs to be paid for by the business. Both inflate your overhead expense pool illogically, creating what is, in essence, a false overhead, an overhead pool of dollars and an overhead rate that does not reflect your indirect costs accurately.

Let's first address that area of the myriad incidental costs of doing business, most of which appear to be too petty to even think about. Unfortunately, they sometimes turn out to resemble the famous "death of a thousand cuts," a fate in which no single cut is serious, but taken in the aggregate, they are most serious.

The High Cost of Incidentals

One of the most common mistakes made in tracking and recording casual or incidental costs is to charge them to overhead as a convenient way to account for them. Alternatively, even when it is your intention to charge them to the right accounts where they belong, because they appear to be of little importance, there is always a temptation to put off recording and posting them at the time they are incurred. When the time comes, finally, to post the charges, many days or even weeks later, it is difficult to recall what projects the charges were for. It is then that the charges are simply dumped into the overhead pool as an inevitable consequence of not having a viable alternative.

Most of these charges appear to be petty enough. Postage charges, for example, are rarely large units of cost. In my own business I incur some postage cost every day. Yesterday, I spent $2.82 at the post office. The day before that it was $5.56, $3.00 the day before that and $3.98 a day earlier than that. That is a grand total of $15.36 that could have been charged to general overhead. If it is a typical week's postage bill, the annual cost is $798.72 added to my overhead. And that does not include the cost of the bulk mailings I do occasionally, which at least doubles the annual postage cost.

Even so, that is not a great sum, and of itself it does not greatly burden my overhead rate. But it is only one of the many small incidental costs that seem to be too small to be concerned with. There are many others.

I have fairly frequent need to use overnight delivery services. It costs $10 to $15, usually, to ship a small parcel that would have cost probably $3 or less by parcel post. Whenever possible, I avoid the necessity to use overnight services. They are satisfyingly convenient, but they are costly. When I am compelled to use them, I usually charge them to my customer's project and recover the costs without burdening my overhead. Even so, these are occasional costs and not as serious as some other incidental costs that tend to become far more serious total expenditures.

For one, there is the telephone bill. Basic telephone service is inescapably a general overhead cost, but the toll calls need not be. They add several thousand dollars a year to overhead for many small businesses. And that is not for voice telephone alone, but also for telephone tolls for fax messages and, in many cases, for online computer usage. Some are for overhead activity, marketing principally, but some are in behalf of specific customers for specific projects and ought to be logged in as direct expenses of the project and paid for by the customer for whom that project was conducted.

There are travel costs, some local and small, some much bigger, involving the use of private automobiles, rental cars, airfares, taxicabs, hotels and meals. Sometimes automobile or rail travel is as fast, in the end, as air travel, and certainly less costly. I always use Amtrak when I travel to New York City these days. It takes me to midtown Manhattan, whereas the air shuttle takes me to a suburban airport, from which I must take a taxi or bus for a total elapsed time equal to that of Amtrak. The air shuttle is actually more troublesome and at least equally expensive, if not even more expensive, in the aggregate. Incidentally, I am often able to have the customer billed directly for all expenses when I travel as part of a direct project function. That conserves my own cash supply and minimizes the overhead costs of interest. Using your credit cards and other charges adds overhead costs. If you incur interest costs, take them into account in getting reimbursed by customers.

There are printing and copying costs, again minor and major for different projects. Depending on the nature of your business, this can become a major cost item. Again, if they are functions of a contracted project, the customer should be paying directly for the printing and copying.

There are subcontracts you let for support of various other kinds, such as consulting, laboratory work, computer programming or other tasks, involving expense on your part for administering and managing the subcontracts.

In the aggregate, these and other costs of this type represent a significant part of your total overhead, even if you count only the smaller items, the "incidentals." Taken together, they can easily be responsible for elevating your overhead costs, and thus your overhead rate, by as much as a third or more. That is, they can be the reason you have an overhead rate of 90 percent instead of 60 percent.

This is not to say that the postage, printing, travel and other items that you use for marketing or administrative purposes should not become overhead items. They are legitimate overhead, incurred for and necessary to the general support of your business. However, the postage, printing, travel and other such costs incurred for direct support of and necessary to specific projects are direct costs, properly, and should not burden your overhead accounts.

True versus False Overhead

Charging all these kinds of items to overhead means, in actuality, that you have created what was referred to earlier as a false overhead. It is false when most of these costs are not true indirect costs. When you mail materials to a customer, the cost of doing so is a direct cost that ought to be chargeable to that customer's account, where and when that is practical. To charge them to your own overhead—to *you*, that is—is handing the customer a generous present, but it is a present at your own cost and unwarranted.

Once again, remember that you must recover all costs, by one means or another. However, there are different ways to recover all costs, and some serve your interests more than do others.

Admittedly, it is much simpler to "absorb" such minor costs by charging them to overhead and setting your rates to cover them. Unfortunately, that has the effect of either forcing you to raise your rates to cover such incidentals (if you are not going to charge them directly), making your marketing a more difficult task, or forcing you to set your profit margins far lower than they ought to be.

A decent profit margin is especially difficult to achieve when you permit sizable costs of such nature to be paid as overhead. If, for example, you incur a large printing bill to complete a given project and pay that bill out of overhead, you make that customer a too-generous present by absorbing costs that customer ought to compensate you for, and you penalize your other customers. Your other customers are paying that large printing bill in the overhead you charge them. You should not have to pay fair project costs out of that portion of the bill you are supposed to be able to keep as your own salary and profit. It's neither fair to yourself nor is it good business practice.

You can combat that problem by the relatively simple expedient of assigning each project, whether it is a simple typesetting job or a major computer programming task, an individual charge number and recording all costs incurred for that project as direct costs against that project, to be billed to that customer.

That method of handling a project is commonly known as "via a T&M or Time and Materials contract." The customer agrees to pay your hourly or daily rate—if it is that type of project or that is the way you customarily quote and charge jobs—and to pay all incidental direct costs, the material costs.

A T&M contract may pose a psychological problem for you if it is not the way you customarily conduct your business. Perhaps what you deliver to your customers is almost entirely service, with associated incidental expenses too minor for concern—or so they appear to you. You fear that your customers will object to any added requirement that they pay for specific incidental items, such as postage, toll calls, fax messages, copying and shipping. It's a groundless fear. It has been my experience that most rarely, if ever, has a customer objected to my being entirely businesslike if I handled my presentation in an objective way with proper preparation and explanation—a subject we will explore further in Chapter 9. We have been discussing how to *set* the rates you need to make a success of your service business. In Chapter 9 we will discuss how to *get* the rates you need. That is largely a matter of proper presentation, a marketing consideration deserving its own discussion.

Unnecessary Overhead Costs

Probably more serious and of much greater magnitude in total costs and in effect on the overhead rate is the problem of recognizing overhead costs that ought not to be incurred in the first place, at least as chargeable business costs. Far too many young, small businesses struggling to grow, if not to merely survive, undertake unwise overhead costs and manage to somehow rationalize them as necessary to the business. A great deal of discipline is required to face the facts that are often harsh disillusionments of fondly held beliefs, based on nothing more than our perceptions—or, perhaps, misperceptions—that some wasteful practices are "how it is done" by other, large corporations. We fail to recognize that many of the practices of large corporations are simply not applicable to the small company. For example, $5,000 may be petty cash not even noticeable in the overhead expense pool of the corporation with a $5 or $10 million overhead burden. That hardly applies to you, with an annual overhead total of perhaps $40,000. The scale makes a great difference.

Large corporations with deep pockets, trying to attract the most able of new employees, often offer rather extravagant blandishments, such as expense-paid travel for interviews, elaborate fringe benefit plans, company-paid social events and sundry other benevolent programs. Small businesses often attempt to emulate such practices, believing that they must do so to be competitive.

The fact is that there is no need to be competitive in this area of business operation. More important, most small businesses cannot afford such refinements, especially not in the early years of their growth to maturity. This is an area where rigid discipline is necessary to exclude from overhead all expenses that cannot be justified as necessary overhead.

Unnecessary luxuries, such as those referred to here, are probably the lesser cause of unnecessary overhead, especially since they tend to be rather obvious as unnecessary expenses. Still, they often do find their way into your overhead pool. There are a number of these types of unnecessary overhead costs commonly encountered. Since they usually tend to be less obviously an unnecessary waste of overhead money, they are often rationalized as they creep into the overhead accounts. They are thus eliminated only with difficulty. Costs associated with marketing represent one fertile area for such waste of overhead money.

Unproductive Marketing Costs

Marketing is without question a critically important function of any business. In fact, it is in my opinion the most important function of business generally, if not of all businesses specifically. It follows that marketing entails expense, and that the expense is justified and necessary generally, although that may not be true in any given case. That is where the problem lies: In a great many cases it is not at all obvious whether a given marketing expense is fruitful or futile, and thus marketing money, usually a major element of overhead, may be wasted, month after month.

Advertising Costs

Advertising is, for a great many businesses, the single most important and most expensive marketing activity. Unfortunately, it is not always easy to ascertain even generally, much less by actual measure, the qualitative or quantitative results of your advertising. You therefore have a difficult time discovering what your return on advertising investment is—that is, whether your money is wasted. One executive was reported quite widely to have said, "I know that one-half of my advertising dollar is wasted, but I don't know which half it is." Of course, quite often it is far more than one-half of the advertising and sales promotional dollars that is wasted because of the typical difficulty in measuring the sales resulting from specific advertisements and promotions.

One aspect of the problem is that most of us do more than one kind of advertising or other sales promotion, so that even when we experience a surge in sales, it is not easy to know which of our marketing initiatives provided the boost. Even when we have not instituted any new marketing programs of any kind, business is subject to peaks and valleys that we cannot anticipate or explain. Sometimes advertising produces immediate results, sometimes it produces results only after long lapses, and sometimes it fails to ever produce substantial results. (I was startled only yesterday to receive an order from a long-ago advertisement that had never worked very well.) Inexplicable ups and downs are manifestations of most kinds of business and most kinds of advertising. For most kinds of advertising or other promotion, you need to utilize special measures to determine how worthwhile it is, in terms of effectiveness and, most importantly, return on investment. It takes specific effort, usually, to get even a general picture of that ROI: Most advertisers never get even a reasonably accurate idea of how well their advertising dollars have paid off. And if you are committed on a long-term basis, as in the case of Yellow Pages advertising, there is not much you can do about it for the rest of that year, even if you discover that your Yellow Pages advertisement is not doing much for you.

Mail Order/Direct Mail Advertising

One kind of advertising can easily be made to be measurable in the results it produces. That is direct mail or mail order advertising. These two terms are commonly used interchangeably, and a great many people use the term "mail order" to refer also to direct mail, but they are not truly identical. The chief distinction lies in how the offer is sent out to the prospect. In mail order, the original offer is made via broadcast advertising, in print most commonly, but also in radio-TV. In direct mail, the original offer is made by mail, by what many call "junk mail" because it so often arrives in a fat envelope stuffed to bursting with letters, brochures and other items intended to help persuade the recipient to become a respondent and place an order. In fact, it is also a common practice to use envelope copy-teasers on the outside of the envelope that herald the contents and try to tempt the recipient to open the envelope in order to see the promised treasures awaiting within.

Keying Your Advertising

It is relatively easy to judge at least in general how well such a campaign is working if you have made a specific offer in it and can identify each order as the result of the advertisement. You do this, generally, by "keying" your advertising, that is, adding something to the advertisement that identifies for you which specific mailing, which print advertisement or which broadcast commercial produced the order. That is why you see instructions to send your order to "Dept. XX2" or some equally cryptic code. Each advertisement, broadcast campaign or sales package carries such an identifier or key that enables the advertiser to determine how the advertising is doing. You can discover in this manner which of your advertisements or promotions is working well and which is not. That enables you to make the wise decisions to cut your losses immediately when you find advertising that does not work well and expand those that do work well.

When you do general advertising of your services, rather than advertising that makes some specific offer to sell something easily identifiable, it is much more difficult to measure the results, even in general. You can ask each new customer where or how he or she learned of your existence, but that provides only the most general of indications and is far from being a reliable method for getting an overall measure.

One way you can address this problem is to plant clues, such as, "Ask for Mr. Murphy when you call," or even, "Ask for Mr. Murphy when you call and get a special discount on your first order." Or: "Tell them Johnny Williams sent you, for a special discount on your first order." You can, of course, also use "Mr. Green," "Mr. Jones" and other names to key each of your advertisements and evaluate the results of each. This is a step forward in measuring results.

Institutional Advertising

Large corporations often do advertising of a kind that is not likely to produce direct results. Mobil Oil or General Electric Company, for example, may run full-page advertisements in national magazines that do nothing but extol their virtues, attest to their importance in the scheme of things, commemorate what they believe to be their grand achievements, and otherwise simply remind the reader that they are important eminences in American industry.

Such advertisements, often referred to as "institutional advertising," probably have some effect on the advertiser's sales when the advertiser sells products or services bought directly by the public at large. Simply making the public more aware of the existence of the advertiser produces some business, of course.

On the other hand, institutional advertising is also utilized by corporations who never sell directly to the public or by corporations who sell only to government and to other corporations. An aircraft manufacturer, such as Boeing, or a major defense contractor, such as General Dynamics, may also indulge themselves in such advertising, for whatever purposes one can only imagine. Certainly, such advertisements do not produce sales for them directly, although they may help a bit by simply reminding their potential customers of their existence.

Small businesses, and even some who are not so small, cannot really afford to do this kind of advertising. Yet, many do, apparently on the premise that simply making one's name and business identity known represents effective advertising. It does not, of course. To be effective, advertising must *sell* something, something *specific*, that is. Otherwise, it is a waste of dollars because it violates one of the basic rules of advertising: You must always answer the prospect's conscious or unconscious question (which even the prospect may not have specifically articulated)—What's in it for me? When you fail to anticipate and answer that presumed question, you give the prospect absolutely no reason to be interested in whatever you offer. (That is, however, a matter we ought properly to address in a later chapter devoted especially to the problem of *getting* the prices you set earlier.)

Sales Promotions

Large organizations often sponsor local events and groups, such as a Little League baseball team. This is very much the same thing as institutional advertising in print or in broadcast media: It puts your name before the public, but does not attempt to sell any specific item or service. It should not cost you more to support a local Little League team or sponsor a bowling team than it costs a large corporation to do so. But while such expenditures are hardly noticeable in an already large overhead expense pool, they can represent a major item of overhead expense to a small business. Such promotions do nothing of note to the overhead rate of the large organization, but they have a great effect on your overhead. A promotion of this type can possibly bring excellent returns, but in most cases the advertising effect is institutional and produces virtually zero business as a direct result. From the strictly practical viewpoint, promotions of this type are a waste of overhead dollars: They produce little in the way of direct results.

This does not mean that all sales promotions are a waste of money. The right kind of sales promotion can be as effective as any paid advertising or even more effective than paid advertising. It can also be and usually is a great deal less expensive. One promotional activity that proves directly beneficial for many small business owners is the complimentary newsletter.

The newsletter is an effective form of direct mail advertising, as well as a promotional device. Its immediate advantage is that it is not "junk mail." Most who receive it will enjoy reading it, if you are careful to tailor it to the probable direct interests of your customers and prospective customers. It is an effective medium for your own tactful advertising, as well as plainly apparent advertising notices in its pages. You can measure your readers' interest by requiring that they request the publication: You send the first issue uninvited and offer a free subscription to all who request it. You may then key items in your newsletter to help you measure results. It becomes your very own advertising medium, combining the characteristics of direct mail, print advertising and sales promotion.

Other promotional items should be considered against the same criteria of possibilities of verifying results by measurement of some sort. One popular promotional item is the logo, an abbreviation of logotype, mentioned earlier (Chapters 2 and 3).

Creating a logo is most often accomplished by hiring a designer to create several ideas for the customer's consideration and settling on one that the designer then develops into a final form.

It is usually an expensive process. The United States Postal Service recently had its logo, an eagle, redesigned. The new eagle was a simpler, starker—and presumably more artistic—presentation than the old eagle. Having the new logo designed and replacing all the earlier logo representations cost the Postal Service a reported amount in excess of $7 million. It did not produce 5 cents' worth of additional revenue, as far as anyone can determine, and despite its efforts to respond to heavy criticism from Congress, the Postal Service was unable to explain why it was necessary to spend $7 million for this process when it was unable to pay its legitimate bills without gratuitous donations of our tax dollars by the Congress.

That predicament is typical of logos generally: The most elaborate, artistic and costly logo does not produce income or enhance income in any way, much as champions of logos rationalize their creation and use as an aid to sales and marketing. Established organizations, especially large ones with profitable operations, can easily afford the luxury of creating a distinctive symbol of this sort, and perhaps when one becomes a General Electric or a Pillsbury Company it is something of an aid to marketing to have a readily recognizable symbol on one's products and advertising. Perhaps. For the fledgling company without an established image, however, it's a self-indulgence and a pure waste of overhead money that would have been put to better use pursuing the next sale.

Location

Many businesses benefit from having a "good address," an address in a prestigious location or prestigious office building. If your specialty is some form of support of the medical profession—health/medical writing services, for example—you may find it a distinct business asset to locate your offices in a building or one of the modern business-condominium complexes that house a number of medical specialists. Or if you are in some line that caters to "the carriage trade," you may find it important to be located where you find the carriage trade and can attract those who expect to pay high rates for what they want and would not, if truth were to be told, have any faith in a purchase that was not expensive. However, to deliberately opt for a prestigious address without some substantial reason for justifying the added expense of a high-rent district is simply burdening your overhead wastefully. Think carefully about where you need to be located and opt for the most economical location that meets your criteria arrived at objectively, if you want to spend your overhead dollars as wisely as possible.

At one time, I rented a rather expensive suite of three large offices at a "good" address on fashionable Connecticut Avenue in downtown Washington, DC. This compelled me to pay a monthly fee to park my automobile in a nearby garage. It meant taking lunches and often dinners at expensive restaurants. It meant also using taxicabs frequently for short trips around town. I was also compelled to pay the equivalent of 13 months' rent because each year I was assessed a penalty in what amounted to approximately an additional month's rent for expenses I never really understood. And it meant, also, that I had to pay property taxes to the District Government, although I did not live there and I did pay taxes on everything I bought there.

It came to quite a burden for a small business, essentially a one-man business, and when the lease came up for renewal, I decided that I could as easily conduct my business out of an office in my own home. And there was an added benefit to a home-based office: It enabled me to write off some of the expenses of my home as a business deduction, reducing my personal expenses. All in all, the home-based office proved to be a splendid idea! It made a quite satisfying reduction in my overhead and spared me that harassing and time-wasting daily commute, as well. Consider the double benefits possible in a home-based business.

Supplies and Equipment

Perhaps you have encountered scratch pads that have something printed on the reverse side. Often enough, they are made of old stationery, expensive old stationery, that has outlived its usefulness and was still available in superabundant quantity. It's the result of the excessive optimism of some entrepreneurs who order a life-time supply of costly letterheads, with matching envelopes and business cards, only to find that their stationery is obsolete before the first year has ended. Often enough, before the first year is over, drastic changes take place in one's business. A change of address and/or telephone numbers, a change of focus or type of services featured and other changes that obsolete existing stationery commonly occur. It's true that in printing, hence in stationery, the economy of scale is a real factor: A ream of stationery (500 sheets) costs a great deal less when it is one of several dozen reams, rather than one alone or one of two. It's a false economy, however, when it's a several-years' supply and is obsolete before the first year ends. (In fact, I no longer have preprinted stationery because I have the capability for creating my own stationery with my normal office equipment. I use a good grade of paper, and my equipment—late-model computer, software and printer—creates professional-looking letterheads spontaneously and on demand. In fact, I now have several letterheads, all residing in my computer, ready to appear on demand. That capability is a great convenience for any-one whose business offers a diverse set of services.

The same reasoning applies to office furnishings, furniture and fixtures. Their usefulness is not linked to their cost—a computer functions as well on a $200 desk as it does on an $800 desk—and you can save a great deal of overhead money by being conservative in all purchasing. That is especially the case if yours is the type of enterprise in which customers rarely visit your premises, as in my own case. I started with completely improvised furniture, furnishings and equipment, and I replaced them with better furniture, furnishings and equipment out of earnings as the business began to grow and mature. Even today, I consider all alternatives before making a decision to buy a new capital item.

Miscellaneous Marketing Expenses

I once spent precious marketing dollars to attend various conventions and trade shows. I enjoyed them thoroughly, but it is expensive to fly off across the country, stay in hotels and take prospects to dinner every night. At one time or another I attended annual conventions and trade shows of *Training* magazine, the Society of American Value Engineers, the National Society for Programmed Instruction, the American Booksellers Association and a number of others. I did this only as long as I could find justification in solid marketing results—sales of my services. When I could no longer verify that I was getting such results from my investments in such activity, I started to forgo the pleasures of these outings.

For many kinds of businesses, it is most important to attend and participate in such events as necessary marketing activities. It is a mistake, however, to do so under the justification that it is "the thing to do" or "it is expected." You should be able to justify such expenditures of your time and money on entirely practical, objective grounds, and you ought to recognize that your time is, of course, money. If you devote three days to attending such a convention or other meeting, and you are paying yourself $40,000/year, three days costs your business $576.92 for your salary alone. But it also costs you for the overhead on three days of salary and for the various expenses of attending the convention. Weigh this against the probable return on that investment to judge whether the expense is money well invested. Apply this acid test: How else might you invest the same amount of money to bring in new business, and how do the probable results of that compare with this contemplated marketing effort? Try to forget the emotional side—the pleasure of the trip and convention—and make as objective an evaluation as possible.

Many business owners invest dollars in promotional novelties inscribed with their names. Among the novelties I myself often receive with the entrepreneur's name plainly inscribed are ballpoint pens, letter openers, calendars, business-card–size calculators, stop watches, clocks, paper clip dispensers, memo pads, portfolios, wallets, flashlights and, I am sure, others that I can no longer recall. (Many appear to be rather expensive throwaway items.) Whether these produce significant new business or not is difficult to say. Frankly, I am skeptical, although I admit to having invested in such items myself a few times. I stopped doing so because I could not find a way to verify that these were worthwhile investments. Perhaps they were, but I had no evidence for it. I think it is wise for the small business owner to contemplate all such investments with a large measure of skepticism and the philosophy, "When in doubt, leave it out"—of the marketing budget, that is. Being "from Missouri"—i.e., skeptical—is not a bad idea in evaluating such items as these. (Some of these ballpoint pens with my name on them were not very good pens, it turned out, and so hardly a testimonial to the excellence of my services.)

Bartering

One excellent way to reduce marketing overhead is by bartering, an increasingly popular way of conducting some of your business. Bartering is one of the oldest ways of conducting trade, of course. In the early days of this country, many frontiersmen subsisted by trapping small game and trading their pelts for flour, bacon, tools, nails and whatever else they needed. (In fact, the John Jacob Astor fortune was built on fur trading.)

Bartering is conducted on the grand scale by large businesses, who find it a practical and convenient way to get rid of surplus inventory, but small businesses find it viable for trading services also. The annual directory of a local barter exchange, Barter Systems, Inc., of Maryland, reveals among its membership many accountants, dentists, lawyers, psychologists, writers, interior decorators, chiropractors, automobile repair shops and other tradespeople.

The typical barter exchange is a community of its own, a community of businesses and professional services, mostly small businesses and independent professionals, but it sometimes includes rather sizable organizations too. (A large appliance store chain in this area has recently joined a local barter exchange.) It is a closed community, in some ways, and especially in this way: Those businesspeople and professionals looking to swap their goods and services will buy first from others who are in that community—who are also willing to swap. That is, accepting the trade credits—dollar values standing to your credit in the accounts of the exchange—gives you a marketing advantage over those who are not barterers and who will accept only dollars for what they sell. The membership of any barter organization you join is a special kind of niche market.

There are more than 400 barter exchanges in the country. Most are individual organizations, but many are branch offices of a chain. Los Angeles–based BXI is probably the largest one, with about 90 offices in 32 states and Puerto Rico, although by far the largest number of BXI offices are in California, followed by the number of exchanges in Florida. Check your Yellow Pages under Barter to find a barter exchange near you (a starter list is included here in the Appendix) and find out what it can mean to you as both a special market opportunity and a help to conserving your cash resources. It is advantageous to join a large barter system, of course, because it is the members of that system who represent that special market. However, most barter systems will cooperate with other barter systems in arranging trades between members of different exchanges.

You normally join a barter exchange and trade with other members of the exchange, using a kind of scrip or a form of checks. The operators of the exchange assist you in making trades—actually, you acquire credits when you sell something and use your credits to buy things. It does a great deal to reduce your marketing costs, while it also helps your cash flow and provides a kind of special niche market represented by all the other traders who belong to your exchange. It's that which helps cut your marketing overhead by a substantial margin. The exchange takes a percentage of the value of each trade.

Among the references furnished later will be a starter list of barter exchanges, where you may learn more about this popular method of trading.

Temping and Subcontracting

Still another way to cut marketing costs sharply is by temping or subcontracting. As in bartering, this is a way of paying commissions or selling your services at a discounted rate to someone acting as a kind of broker and finding work for you, so that the discounts you allow or commissions you pay out constitute your marketing expense.

This subject will come up again in the next chapter, in discussing rates and estimating. Briefly, this approach usually involves working on a customer's premises at some fixed hourly rate. There are many brokers with work to offer freelance workers or independent contractors (also often considered to be independent consultants). You may be able to get much of this kind of work by contracting directly with the customer, but that entails the usual marketing expenses: Time, advertising and other associated expenses. On the other hand, getting this kind of work through a middleman or broker entails little effort or time and expense on your part, and many independent contractors manage to stay busy by engaging in this kind of activity, with the benefit of relatively little money spent on marketing.

Chapter 8

Developing Accurate Estimates

Estimating is a necessary and quite important part of any service or other custom business. It is, in fact, almost always more art than science or method, requiring one to predict not only the amount of effort required but the probability of Murphy's Law—the unpredictable and pernicious problems that will inevitably appear at the most inopportune time possible.

Why Estimating Is a Necessity

Estimating the effort and costs of a potential project to perform custom work of any kind is rarely easy, and the new prospective project rarely resembles a former project as closely as it may seem to at first. You may get a sense of deja vu when you first contemplate a new inquiry because certain aspects and features are familiar. The task seems rather familiar, and as you begin to study the task, it more and more seems to resemble some project of the past, and your confidence grows steadily, in the belief that this project will be duck soup for you. You are tempted to assure the customer that you know exactly what he or she needs and can furnish a close estimate with little delay and with a great sense of assuredness.

That cocksureness can be and probably will be a dangerous beginning: Such "surefire" projects often turn out to be Loreleis, luring you onto the rocks of disaster. Most service businesses are essentially custom work, and only rarely does a new project come close to being exactly like some previous project, no matter how closely it may appear at first glance. In a service business, each project is almost without exception somehow unique and often full of surprises you could not have anticipated (most unpleasant surprises, that is), hence the need for and the difficulty of estimating carefully and with great thought. You do well to make it a rule that *every* new project must be carefully estimated.

The hazard of unpleasant surprises and the difficulty of anticipating all the possible pitfalls are the chief reasons for the pronounced tendency of those conducting small service businesses to prefer quoting and working by the hour at a stipulated hourly rate. This practice greatly lessens that need for and difficulty of estimating projects, or so it appears. An hourly rate thus imparts a much greater sense of security, as was noted earlier, or it at least appears to be an easier way of estimating than alternative methods. The reasoning process, probably an unconscious or semiconscious one, is that there is far less hazard of underestimating the project and risking losses when one quotes and works by the hour, rather than by a fixed price for the job. Trying to anticipate problems is difficult, and the relative finality of a fixed price appears to be a great potential hazard. But an hourly rate appears to be more open-ended and thus less hazardous, whether or not it is so, in fact. The apprehension is understandable, of course, as is the need to feel a sense of security. As we proceed to examine and consider the subject of estimating, we will consider the pros and cons of furnishing fixed-price estimates versus those of furnishing hourly rates. I will also offer you some suggestions on how to reduce the hazards, apparent and real, of underestimating your projects, so that you will have a higher level of confidence in your estimates.

Is the Hourly Rate Truly Advantageous?

In my own consulting experience, I have most often quoted and worked by the day, at a fixed daily rate. That is not different, in principle, from working by the hour, except that it implies to the customer that my day rate will be the same for each and every day, regardless of the number of hours I work in a day. I recognized that implication rather early in my consulting experience, and so I did two things about it. 1. I set a day rate high enough to compensate me adequately, even if many of the days I worked proved to be rather long days. (That is a common need in proposal work, especially as the due date approaches because proposal schedules are usually rather short ones and are almost always totally inelastic. Probably no document is quite as useless as the proposal that didn't get delivered on time.) 2. I also turned that necessity and possible disadvantage into an advantage that helped me greatly in closing my sales, but more on that subject in the next chapter.

Despite those stipulations of a fixed day rate and my guarantee that my day rate would never change during the life of the project, my customers wanted reliable estimates of how many days I expected to need to get the job done. The fact of a day rate did not relieve me of the necessity to furnish my customer some degree of commitment on the total cost of my services for the project under discussion. You must remember that you are not alone in your need to have some sense of security: The customer has the same need and therefore wants a good idea of the maximum cost of the project. Few customers will issue you a blank check to charge as many hours or days as you wish!

Thus, charging on the basis of an hourly rate, rather than by a "for the job" fixed price, may seem less risky but really does not change basic requirements greatly. You still must estimate the amount of time and effort required and any routine or extraordinary expenses you anticipate you will incur in getting the job done.

Pros and Cons of the Hourly Rate

There are, of course, cases where the hourly rate is inescapable, either because the customer mandates it as a condition or circumstances render it the only practical way to charge for your work. If, for example, you work a regular business workday on the customer's premises as a virtual temporary or contract employee, there is little alternative to working at an hourly rate. (In fact, in such circumstances, some customers have actually required the contractor to punch a time clock, along with regular employees.)

There are different situations in which you may be working on the customer's premises during regular business hours: One is the situation where you have signed a contract directly with the customer, wherein rates and conditions are specified. These may be take-it-or-leave-it conditions specified by the customer, terms you have been asked to suggest, or terms you have arrived at through negotiations.

There is another, rather common, case where you may sign with a third party, a supplier of services to be provided on the customer's premises. You are technically the employee of the third party, who is a labor broker (often referred to as a "job shop") and who assigns you to work on his or her customer's premises. This is, again, a quite common condition today. The "temporary" is no longer necessarily a typist, secretary or file clerk; temporaries today include many professionals, paraprofessionals, craftsmen and craftswomen, and many other skilled and professional careerists.

At times, as a variant of the latter case, you may be a subcontractor to the third party, rather than an employee, but still be assigned to the customer's premises and working at an hourly rate. The IRS appears to be quite unhappy with this arrangement, and more and more such brokers have felt compelled to become employers of those they would have preferred to engage as subcontractors because that is usually a more desirable set of conditions for all parties but the IRS. Just why the IRS is so adamantly opposed to independent workers becoming contractors or subcontractors working on a customer's premises has never been clear, but the wording of certain federal statutes apparently authorizes their position. Efforts are currently under way to persuade Congress to enact remedial legislation.

An Important Issue: What You Have Contracted To Deliver

Many individuals in the services industries refuse to work on any customer's premises as a temporary employee of either the customer or a labor broker, and many others refuse to work on a customer's premises under any conditions. They see it as a negation of their valued independence, regardless of what the IRS thinks. Others will accept such assignments only if they have no other business available. Of course, others also prefer to work that way, seeing its advantages. This is, of course, an individual decision you must make. That aside, there are some advantages to working at an hourly rate, while still being technically self-employed and independent (although such conditions of work admittedly place you in a gray and shadowy area between being an employee and being an independent contractor). But wait, there is at least one other consideration here: It is in the definition of what you have contracted for—what you have agreed to deliver—and it is at the heart of this part of the discussion.

The IRS regulators are mistrustful of subcontracting where they suspect it is actually a disguise for temporary employment. They have argued that the practice permits the employer to avoid withholding taxes from the employee's salary and jeopardizes the collection of income taxes from the individual. The IRS has therefore employed some standards by which to judge whether the individual is a true subcontractor or is actually a temporary employee from whom taxes should be withheld. One of these standards involves the question of *what* the individual is to deliver under the contract: Has the individual contracted to deliver a specified end product?

So subcontracting—i.e., agreeing to deliver some clearly defined product, even if it is an intangible, such as a report or a computer program, is one indicator of true subcontracting. Where there is no such definition as the objective of the subcontract—i.e., where the subcontractor will simply supply some defined services for as long as the customer wishes to buy the services, it casts serious doubt on the status of the individual as a valid subcontractor. It suggests strongly that the individual is an employee, albeit temporary.

That consideration of a specified end product also has a great impact on the risk involved in estimating your rate, of course. If you are obligated to deliver some specified end product or end result for a specified price or its equivalent (i.e., some number of hours of work at a specified rate), you undertake some estimating risk. You are obligated to deliver that product, even if so doing entails more hours than you estimated or incurs some unexpected expense. On the other hand, if you are obligated only to work a daily number of hours at some specified task or in some specified capacity but with no end product or end result specified, there is no risk: You will be paid for each hour you work, per the agreement.

Estimating Need To Negotiate Hourly Rates

Unless you have a fixed and unvarying rate for any and all situations, you will need to do a little estimating and negotiating even to settle on an hourly rate. Some customers, especially the larger organizations who use such services as yours regularly, may have fixed rates they offer and from which they will rarely, if ever, vary. But that is not true of most customers. Most have some idea of what rates they ought to pay but are prepared to negotiate.

You need, therefore, to anticipate a probable negotiation, whether formal or informal, and to be prepared for it. Preparation to negotiate means advance estimating of what rate you can command and should seek. But there is a bit more than that to deciding, at least in principle, what your negotiating posture is to be. It is likely that if your customer makes you an initial offer, rather than asking you for a quotation, his or her offer will be for the lowest rate possible. That probably, but not necessarily, means that the rate is negotiable, and it is probably possible to do somewhat better than the customer's first offer. If, however, the customer initiates negotiations by asking you to quote a rate, you will want to make it as high a rate as possible to establish your starting position. In either case, there will probably be some negotiation, based on both parties' estimates and limits. You will thus need to estimate how high a rate you can seek, as well as decide for what minimum rate you will settle. It is always wise to begin a negotiation with these limits in mind, rather than being forced to form judgments and make decisions while under the pressure of arguments and counterarguments, even if you may have to adjust these limits as a result of the negotiation.

Thus, the true argument for accepting an hourly rate is the risk-free nature of working that way in situations where you are not committed to some specified end product, as one advantage, but that does not mean that you will never have to negotiate, unless you wish to risk losing sales by maintaining a rigid rate requirement. There is also what I consider to be the somewhat dubious advantage of making your mind a bit easier when you have estimated a project on the basis of an hourly rate, rather than on the basis of time, materials and other expenses. However, it is perhaps a bit easier to estimate a project on an hourly basis, especially when you have some fixed and unvarying rate or rates you charge for your services. That requires a bit of explanation, for which a brief digression is necessary.

A Scale of Varying Rates

Some contractors have one fixed, unvarying rate for whatever they do, while others have a scale of rates for various services. This practice of having different rates for different services can be justified easily, although you may find both customers and vendors who disagree with that idea. Customers tend to have the notion that your time is worth some fixed amount, regardless of the type of work you are doing. The customer may demand to know why your time in writing or illustrating something is worth more than your time in editing or proofing something. You may have set those rates by determining what the market—what your competitors charge—is for each of those types of services, but the customer is unmoved by that. In the next chapter, we shall discuss how to handle such difficult objections, but for now let us note simply that you are justified in making such distinctions and in having a set of rates geared to the nature of the work itself. Still, this can pose a problem when the customer requires that you furnish a detailed cost/price analysis, an increasingly common demand today. One of my purposes here is to help you prepare yourself to meet such demands. We shall get to this presently. However, in the meanwhile, if it is your choice to set a scale of fixed rates for different kinds of work or services, it is necessary to be absolutely clear in defining both the rates and the functions. This may appear to be an obvious and unnecessary injunction, but experience suggests otherwise—i.e., that the explanations of the various functions and rates are not easily apparent merely by the names assigned them and often do require detailed explanation or definition. Take the simple function of editing.

Defining Rates and Functions

At one time I was asked by someone I knew in the Public Buildings Service of the federal government's General Services Administration to quote the cost of editing a manuscript for a brochure the agency wished to make an official document of the Service. I examined the draft manuscript and hesitated. I perceived what the manuscript really needed was extensive rewriting, not editing, according to my own understanding of writing and editing as editorial functions. Still, the distinction between writing a revision and editing is not clear-cut. In fact, one could easily defend making a distinction between "light editing" and "heavy editing" and still have difficulty in defining the dividing point. I therefore felt amply justified in agreeing to a "heavy edit," while quoting the customer for what I planned as a complete revision and rewrite. We were both satisfied: The customer was satisfied that I agreed to "edit" the copy, and he found my price acceptable; I was satisfied that the customer agreed to pay me what I thought the work was worth.

This happened to be a project that I would perform in my own office with my own equipment and facilities, as I usually prefer to do, and so I had no difficulty in quoting this as a fixed-price job, normally my preferred method of working. Otherwise, I might have had the difficulty of justifying writing rates for what the customer deemed to be an editing job. That suggests one of the possible difficulties of using hourly rates in estimating and charging. It can place you in awkward situations in estimating and quoting. The customer is usually a layperson in the craft you practice and has no idea (except a naive one, perhaps) of what is required to do what you do. To the customer's untrained ideas and judgment of the work you do, your stipulation of perhaps eight hours for what the customer thinks to be a minor job might seem to be a grossly exaggerated estimate. That is due in large part to the customer's misunderstanding of what is normally required to get the job done. I have found that often the problems of a customer disagreeing with what one proposes is due to the customer's unfamiliarity with the work. A few minutes spent to "educate" a customer is usually a good investment.

Overcoming Pitfalls in Estimating

What most customers do not perceive is that doing the specific work that is the basis for your service is not doing the entire job you have undertaken. An editing or writing job that might require eight hours to write or edit cannot be estimated and quoted as an eight-hour project. That is because there are usually stages in such work, a first stage discussing the project with the customer to gain a good understanding of the requirement as the customer sees it, then a draft writing or editing for the customer's review, and then final work in response to the customer's review and comments. That series of stages to get a project completed is characteristic of many, if not most, custom projects.

Unfortunately, unless you happen to know the customer, you may occasionally be surprised unpleasantly to find that more than one review and revision is necessary before you have managed to satisfy a given customer and be able to bill for the work. Doing work for a bureaucratic organization, such as a government agency or a large corporation, often entails much more time spent in such matters than in the actual work. I found it necessary to include generous estimates of time required for meetings, discussions and multiple reviews and revisions when doing a project for government agencies, although large associations and other organizations also tend to bureaucratic practices.

I soon learned to ask certain questions up front before quoting such jobs. I asked how many reviews and approving signatures the job required and if there were some final approval by a higher-up required. Of course, if more than one individual had to review and approve a job, the time needed for those meetings and revisions grew in some proportion to the number of reviewers. In one case, 15 signatures were required for a job for the Federal Aviation Administration. It soon became apparent that it would be impossible to create something that all reviewers would approve, as an endless round of reviews and revisions mounted. It resulted, finally, in an appeal from the Contracting Officer for my help in finding a way to somehow conclude the project without getting involved in the difficult legal technicalities of a formal cancellation of a government contract! The contracting official was grateful for my cooperation in closing out a difficult situation, but it could have been anticipated by the mere fact that 15 individuals had to be satisfied, a difficult undertaking at best.

There are sometimes projects you undertake that you wish you had never heard of, let alone contracted to carry out. If you are prudent, when you know nothing of the customer, you will assume that you will spend probably as much or nearly as much time in such peripheral activities as you did doing the primary work. Certainly, you ought never to expect to complete a 20-hour project in

20 hours total project time. You must allow a margin of time for the several time-consuming tasks that are necessary in most projects to get them wrapped up, even after the primary work is completed. However, it is better by far to take steps to learn as much as you can of the customer and his or her organization. Asking the questions posed earlier, as tactfully as possible, of course, is one step in the right direction. But there are often other steps you can take that may prove helpful in making your estimate. One is to be alert for signs of the difficult customer. Here are some signs I found to be significant indicators of customers to be wary of and perhaps to discourage by asking for an extraordinarily high price:

1. The customer who makes it clear in the initial discussion, whether by telephone, face-to-face, or other means of communication, that price is the first, second and probably final consideration. The signal revealing this probability is that he or she opens by asking your rate as virtually the first topic of discussion. This customer will prove to be a tough one to deal with, in all probability, demanding and unforgiving—if, in fact, you can manage to close a deal with him or her at all. In my experience, it seemed to be best to keep my discussion with such a customer as short as possible and hope that we did not succeed in closing a sale!

2. The customer who never asks the price. That is against all logic, but there are such customers. It usually signals that you are wasting your time with someone who will not place an order, but is merely shopping about, has nothing better to do or is picking your brains. However, it may also mean that you will never get paid for anything you do for this party. Ask for a retainer to verify this quickly.

3. The customer who assures you that price is no object. Nonsense. Price is always an object. This customer is probably a variant of the customer described above in the number 2 position.

4. The customer who asks many technical questions and avoids discussing a potential project. This one is almost certainly trying to use you as an unpaid consultant, picking your brains in a literal sense.

5. The customer who complains about your competitors who, he or she claims, did a terrible job for him or her at some past time, who charges too much, is not very good or is otherwise an object of scorn. It is hardly necessary to tell you why this one will be a great headache of a customer.

6. The customer who wants an estimate in writing with full details—a technical proposal, that is, but is rather vague about whether or not a contract is likely to result. That is sometimes another case of picking your brains. Along with many others, I have been the victim of this practice: Having submitted a highly detailed proposal to a large company, I soon found that they had hired someone at a relatively small salary and given him my proposal as his work plan to carry out the project they wanted and for which they had invited my proposal.

You can and should also "ask around"—make inquiries of others you know in your field, such as fellow members of your trade association—especially if you have some misgivings about this customer. See if you can find others who have done business with that customer and can advise you. Some customers achieve a kind of notoriety for possessing some of the characteristics listed above.

The Basis for Your Hourly Rates

There are at least four general standards that have been offered so far for setting your hourly rates:

1. Decide how much money you wish to make.

2. Determine what "the market" is in your service area.

3. Determine what the traffic will bear.

4. Set your own standards for the rates you merit.

The first idea is patently impracticable. Setting your rates on the basis of how much money you wish to make is attempting to meet a purely arbitrary goal that is not really within your power to determine, except as it meets or operates within the constraints of standards 2 and 3 above. In practice, most practitioners' rates reflect items 2, 3 or both and, in a few cases, 4. For our purposes here, therefore, the option listed as number 1 is excluded from further consideration.

The market, as the area practitioners view it, is probably the chief influence in setting any given practitioner's rates. By far the majority of practitioners set their rates in emulation of what they perceive to be the market in the area—i.e., what the customers for such services have come to expect and accept when they require services.

To get rates well in advance of—higher than—rates considered to be representative of the local market is not an unusual feat at all. A great many practitioners are able to do so. Nominally, they are able to do so because they offer superior skills/experience/judgment or another important capability. In fact, they may or may not offer capabilities that are superior in quality. It may be that they have done a superior marketing job, one that persuades prospective customers that the services and capabilities offered are of greatly superior quality. In fact, it appears to me that most of the time it is marketing skill that is the chief reason for one marketer's ability to command much higher prices than another.

I read an appeal this morning on CompuServe from a woman starting a resume-writing service. She reports that her friends are shocked that she asks the princely sum of $20 per hour for her services. Four other writers responded immediately with shock that she had set her rates so low, and at least one made a point of telling her that flat rates for what she does would usually be more palatable to most prospects than any hourly rate would be. Sage advice.

That is the essence of marketing: The customer's perception becomes the fact, the truth and the means for getting top rates for your services. Shaping that perception of the customer is a subject scheduled for the next chapter, so we will not explore it now. Here, we will merely note that you can create your own "market" (read "value of") for your services with the right approaches to the problem. That is, there may not be 5 cents' worth of real difference between the services of John Smith and those of Fred Jones, but one may command $150 per hour, while the other can command only $60 per hour. Why the great discrepancy? It's marketing payoff, purely marketing payoff. One of these specialists has accepted the local market, while the other has set about creating his own market. Which, do you suppose, is the one settling for the "competitive" rate and which is the one finding customers to pay him the higher rate?

Start by Finding Your Minimum Rate

I suggest that one principle to follow in setting your rates is to first determine what your minimum acceptable rate is. You need to take several steps in doing this, not necessarily in this order:

1. Calculate your probable minimum expenses—rent, heat, light, insurance, taxes, equipment, supplies and other— and do so realistically.

2. Estimate the capitalization of your business. Even if you are not investing a significant amount of cash, even if you are planning to use your own automobile, computer, furniture and other capital, you must account for the value of these items as initial investment. You may be able to "expense" these immediately—charge them off as tax deductions in the first year—or you may find it better to depreciate them over a number of years. You probably ought to consult an experienced CPA or other experienced executive whose judgment you trust.

3. Estimate the number of hours of whatever you think will be your normal workweek (not necessarily a 40-hour one) that will be billable to customers.

4. Estimate your operating expense.

5. Determine the minimum income you must have.

The total of items 4 and 5, divided by the number of item 3, then represents the lowest hourly rate you can accept.

That sum is not necessarily the figure to shoot for, of course, but it does put a floor under your calculations and helps you perceive the truth at all times. Otherwise, you might think vaguely that you can muddle through somehow at any rate. But quantifying—creating and estimating actual figures—takes most of the guesswork and misleading intuition (which is too often wishful thinking, rather than true intuition) out of the equation. It helps you keep your feet on the ground.

The figures are themselves estimates, of course, and so are not graven in stone. Reexamine them and recast them often, as experience replaces your best guesses. Compare the minimal hourly rates you arrive at with any other standard or method for setting rates and adjust them upward accordingly—always upward and never downward. They are the *minimum.*

The Written Presentation

Depending on the kind of business you conduct and your methods for conducting it, you may or may not have occasion to prepare written estimates for prospective customers. "Written estimates" include quotations, bids and proposals. These terms are used rather loosely and interchangeably in the everyday business world, but strictly speaking, they are not the same instruments. What follow are more precise definitions for these terms.

Quotation The quotation is usually a response to a request for price information only about some specific service or set of services. Neither the request nor the quotation are binding on either party, and the request may have been issued to one or more respondents. The requester may or may not place an order based on the quotation. Customers issuing many requests for quotations may have a printed form on which they request responses to be submitted. But often a simple memorandum or letter is an adequate medium for response to a request, although you may wish to devise a form of your own.

Bid   The bid is normally a response to a serious request from a prospective customer who has invited more than one party to respond, and who will award an order or contract to one of the bidders, probably, although not necessarily, the lowest bidder. A bid is normally considered to be binding as a serious commitment by the bidder. As in the case of requests for quotation, the customer may supply a written form for responses or request a response in whatever form you choose to make it. Again, you may wish to devise a printed form of your own, where the customer does not supply one.

Proposal   The proposal may take many forms. Typically, it is in response to a request from a prospective customer who has not fully solidified what he or she wants or needs but can only describe the need in general terms—perhaps as a set of symptoms—and wants the respondents to offer their proposed solution and a price. The requester normally retains the right to choose that proposal he or she finds most appealing, price not necessarily the most important factor. It can be as simple a presentation as a price quotation and an illustrative brochure, or it can be a substantial, custom-written volume of many pages. Not all proposals are formally requested by a prospective customer. The proposal may also be submitted as an unsolicited proposal, at the option of the proposer. Customers may stipulate form and content of responses or may leave those matters to respondents.

Where a customer has requested a quotation, bid or proposal, the customer may request that responses be in terms of hourly rates, may leave the basis of the prices up to you or may specify a mixture of some items as hourly rates and some as unit rates of some other kind. A customer for editorial services, for example, may want hourly rates for editorial tasks of several kinds—e.g., writing, editing, illustrating—but ask for per-page rates for typing and proofreading. Even so, you are not precluded from volunteering a second set of rates on a basis of your own choice. Make sure that this is a second set, the first set being completely responsive to the customer's request.

Fixed-Price or Flat-Rate Estimates

The alternatives to hourly rates are the fixed-price and flat-rate methods of estimating and/or pricing your work. These are not the same thing, although they are related to each other. Depending on the kind of work you do, you may have occasion to use either or both methods. If you can use both, you will have an advantage of great flexibility. It is possible that you can or must use hourly rates also, in some situations, further increasing your flexibility in estimating, quoting and pricing. For this discussion, however, we will focus entirely on fixed prices and flat rates, although we shall return to hourly rates in a later discussion in this chapter.

Hourly rate estimates are the simplest kinds of cost presentations, usually, although there are occasional exceptions to this. A simple project may require merely a price for the entire project—e.g., 65 hours at $35 per hour or $2,275. Occasionally, even the hourly rate request may be relatively complex, as Figure 8.1 should illustrate. This is a rather small "laundry list." More often, these kinds of procurements involve many more services than these and even more complex distinctions among the many categories of services, but the principle is the same.

Figure 8.1   **A Typical Small "Laundry List" Bid or Quotation**

Service/Function	Rate/Hour: $	Rate/Page: $
Writing	38	
Editing	27	
Illustrating	25	
Typing		3.00
Proofreading		2.50

Frequently, some of the categories do require somewhat detailed classifications or descriptions. Writing alone is widely varied in its demands, qualifications and, therefore, costs. Technical writers are likely to command higher hourly rates than general writers because the demands and qualifications of technical writing are usually far more specialized. But even within the overall category of technical writing there are specialties. There are technical writers who specialize in writing about computer technology, those who specialize in writing maintenance manuals for equipment, those whose chosen forte is radar or avionics, and those who write about space and missiles. There are many specialties, and the specialty may be in the type of written product, the kinds of equipment, or other parameters—military manuals, mainframe computers, software manuals, communications equipment, corporate documents (personnel manuals, purchasing procedures or fringe benefit studies), and almost countless other areas and kinds of specialization. (Many of these specialized writers are, in fact, special consultants, as well as technical writers.) Some writers claim to be able to handle all these subjects, but many customers demand specialists with special qualifications for their projects, and prices are dictated by this factor, as well as others. As a general rule of thumb, the more demanding the customer is, with regard to special qualifications, the higher the rate the client must be and presumably is prepared to pay. That means, of course, the higher the rate you are entitled to demand and get. That is part of the upside of specialization.

Higher rates for specialized services are not peculiar to writing or editorial services, of course. Those were used as a convenient reference to illustrate the principle. That principle would apply equally to any other kind of service. Were the service engineering, it might include various kinds of engineering and sundry engineering tasks. Were it to apply to computer services, it would include a variety of kinds of computer services and kinds of computer specialists. And that would apply equally to information brokerage, supply of temporaries, legal and paralegal services, accounting services, mailing list services, therapeutic services, and a wide, almost unlimited, variety of other services and functions. The principle has almost universal application.

Flat-Rate Estimates and Pricing

The quotation shown in Figure 8.1 was a flat-rate kind of estimate because even the hourly rates shown were of that nature, since they were commitments to a given rate per unit of time. This type of quotation is ordinarily for "open-ended" or "indeterminate quantity" contracts. These are contracts under which the customer may order services as needed, usually by issuing a task order and asking the contractor to estimate the service needed under the enabling contract—i.e., as specified. You may then negotiate the task with the customer, if he or she does not agree with your estimate of the services required. The negotiation, in such cases, is about what services and what quantities of those services are required, not the cost of the services because the costs were defined in the enabling contract. You can see that with such an "open-ended" contract—representing an attempt to predict all the probable requirements of the next year, although some of them are multiyear contracts—the number and types of services are usually more numerous than those of Figure 8.1.

The Rate Problem of Multiyear Contracts

That issue of multiyear contracts raises another problem concerning rates: The problem of inflation and cost/price increases. One has difficulty today predicting this year's probable costs, hence setting rates, let alone trying to anticipate future years' rises in costs and rates resulting from cost increases. Thus, in estimating a multiyear contract, one must include some factor for inflationary increases and some standard for invoking raises.

Usually, one estimates a percentage increase in costs and rates, possibly on the order of 3 to 5 percent. If pressed to justify such increases, one may invoke the federal government's published "CPI" or cost/price index.

Fixed-Price Estimates and Pricing

Either or both hourly and flat-rate estimates may be used to develop fixed-price estimates in order to price your services. If you have established flat-rate and/or hourly rates for all functions you offer to perform for customers, your estimating task is one of deciding which of your regular services you need and how much of each. If you have no standard or specified service categories and rates but develop a custom estimate from scratch for each new project, you will have to decide for each project precisely what services/functions are required to carry out the various duties and tasks of the project and how much of each you will need.

That may, of course, require a mix of your standard rates and functions for part of the project, together with new rates and functions you devise for the new project. If you seek only sizable projects that normally require bids and proposals to pursue, you are likely to encounter needs for which you have to devise functions and set rates.

The Project Estimating Process

Whichever the case, you will normally have to do several things to develop your estimate(s). Following is a suggested process:

1. Analyze the requirement as best you can from the information available to you. (The customer's description of the need may or may not be adequately clear and detailed for your need. In some cases, you may have to be a resourceful investigator to gather all the necessary information.)

2. Develop a general plan of attack, a procession of functions and services necessary to achieve the customer's aims. (I have found it extremely helpful to develop a block diagram/

flow chart laying out this succession of functions in their logical order. See Figure 8.2 for an example of a flow chart depicting the flow of phases and functions in the typical proposal development process.)

3. Develop that into a detailed plan, with various phases and functions clearly defined.

4. Quantify those phases and functions necessary to carry out the project.

5. Price those phases and functions you have defined, plus price any incidental costs you project as necessary project expenses.

At that point you have collected an estimate for the project in terms of the direct labor you require and, if appropriate, necessary other costs. You can now add all other factors of overhead, other

Figure 8.2 **A Typical Block Diagram/Flow Chart**

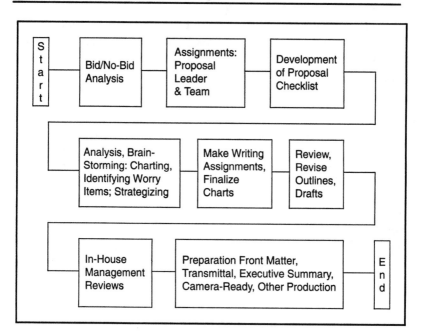

direct costs, if any, G&A, if any, and fees or profit. You can prepare a written estimate now, in the general format of Figures 5.1 through 5.4 or in a similar format. Of course, you need not supply this to your customer. (You have no need to, nor should you reveal these details of your business to anyone but your accountant and, perhaps, the IRS. The exception is when you are contracting with a government agency or subcontracting to a government contractor on a sizable project where the government requires that information.) However, you should do this for your own information to develop accurate estimates.

However you do your basic estimate, but especially if you estimate by some seat-of-the-pants method—"gut feelings," for example—try developing a second estimate by some other method, one that is completely independent of the first method, and be sure to develop that flow chart for all but the simplest projects. Then compare the estimates. (I have long made it a practice to do this.) You may very well find a substantial difference between the two estimates, and it is often enough that the higher of the two is the more accurate one. If the two are close, on the other hand, it should greatly increase your confidence in your estimate.

There is a Step 6 that I did not include in the sequence of steps outlined earlier on pages 158–159 because I thought it best to introduce it here, after discussing the basic estimating processes. It is this:

6. Compare your estimate with "the market."

If you are unsure of what typical prices might be for such a project, ask around. Check with any professional associates you have, with friends in the same business, with fellow members of an association you belong to, with online companions of a service, such as CompuServe and America Online, or by whatever means you can devise to gather market intelligence. (I do hope that you have such means as an essential part of your marketing.) You are going to find one of three possible conditions:

1. Your price is about in line with the market—what you might expect most of your competitors to quote.

2. Your price is significantly higher than the market.

3. Your price is significantly below the market.

The third condition should set alarm bells ringing. If your price is well under the market, is it because you underestimated the job? Is it because you are working too cheaply? Or is it because you have so equipped and trained yourself that you are more efficient than most of your competitors?

Consider raising your price, of course, to at least the average of the market. Even if you have not underestimated the job, you should not be the cheapest guy in town, not only because you are denying yourself the fruits of what you have done to make yours an optimum service, but because cheapest guy in town is not a reputation that helps your business to become well recognized as a quality service and to grow.

If you are about on the level of the market, you should also consider raising your price. If you do this, you will risk pricing yourself out of the job, of course. But it is a certain, low-priced market out of which you are pricing yourself. Bear that in mind always: There are *many* markets, and you must choose the one in which you wish to compete.

The risk of pricing yourself higher than your competitors depends on your clear view of who your competitors really are: Are they the rank and file who are charging rates dictated by competitors (for that is how most "standard" rates come into being)? Or are they your real competitors, the few who charge much more than most do and satisfy their customers that what they provide is worth what they charge? You should, by now, have decided who your real competitors are and be competing on the basis of excellence of your service and your skills in marketing.

Finally, if you find that your estimated price is already well above that of your lower-priced competitors, analyze why that is. Have you overestimated the job or is it about right for what you do that is superior to what most others do? How does your price compare with that of your real competitors? Decide, finally, whether it is the right price, all factors considered?

Estimating Tips and Techniques

Far too many small business owners estimate projects they are bidding for by the seat of their pants—by intuition or by what they hope is reliable instinct. Perhaps that works most of the time, but certainly it does not work all of the time, and only one disastrous mistake in estimating and bidding is enough to put a small business in great jeopardy. Aside from getting the best price, one must also worry about getting the minimum price acceptable. In short, something better than seat of the pants is needed for analyzing a sales opportunity and bidding well: One needs a *method* or two.

The Flow-Chart Method

The development and use of a flow chart for estimating is extremely useful, I have found, for projects of any complexity, even relatively simple ones. The example of Figure 8.2 is that of a relatively generalized functional flow diagram of the proposal process, identifying major functions. Each block identifies one or more functions that can be broken down into many actions, and it is sequential, listing the order in which functions and processes should be carried out. To create such a chart, you must analyze the customer's statement of work (that which the requester of a proposal normally supplies to guide you in responding). But it is up to you to break that statement of work down into the specific tasks and functions necessary to get the job done. Developing a detailed flow chart is an effective means of helping you think out the entire project and all its requirements. For example, the bid/no-bid analysis is necessary to decide whether you will or will not submit a proposal. (Only if you so decide, are the second and other succeeding blocks germane.) From that point on, the chart simply identifies the things you must do to develop a proposal for submittal.

The chart in Figure 8.2 was developed to describe a process. For purposes of analyzing the needs of a project and estimating the effort and related costs necessary to carry it out, a more detailed functional flow chart is required. Let us take, as a simple example, the first block alone. A customer has invited you to submit a proposal for a certain project. Let us see what are some of the criteria for making a judgment:

- Is the prospective project for the kind of work you normally do?

- Do you believe yourself to be in a good competitive position?

- Do you have the capacity for producing a powerful proposal?

- Do you need the contract?

- Is it work you really want to do?

- Do you believe you have a truly good chance for success?

All of these are variables. The contract opportunity you might have spurned a year ago may be an attractive project today, according to your current situation—i.e., how badly you need a new contract. That concern alone can be a decisive factor in your decision making. However, the logic of a functional flow chart is the "how?"–"why?" logic: Each block should answer "why" in the next block and "how" in the preceding block. Let's test this by applying it to Figure 8.2.

Why make the bid/no-bid analysis? So we can get on with it and assign the proposal leader and team. Why make those assignments? So we can develop the proposal checklist. Etc. In reverse: How do we develop the proposal checklist? By assigning a proposal leader and team. Etc.

The why-how rationale is much clearer when the flow chart addresses the project in greater (lower level) detail than in this example, but it always applies as the rationale for a proper functional flow chart. It validates the legitimacy of any flow chart, but it is also—and more importantly—the guide for developing a functional flow chart. Use it in analyzing a requirement, whether you do or do not actually chart it, although I recommend that you do. However, an alternative is available, if you prefer one.

The Outline Method

It is possible to use the why-how approach without actually chart-ing it by implementing the idea in outline form. You can then use this directly as an aid to estimating the project, or you can use it as a guide to flow charting—i.e., you can convert the outline to a flow chart. Here is the beginning of the chart of Figure 8.2 as an outline:

I. BID/NO-BID ANALYSIS

II. ASSIGNMENTS
   A. Proposal leader
   B. Team members

III. DEVELOPMENT OF PROPOSAL CHECKLIST

You can probably see from this the significance of the "why" and "how" questions and the amount of detail you can add, as you develop this more fully by breaking down and explaining each of these major heads and subheads. For example:

I. BID/NO-BID ANALYSIS
   A. Criteria
     1. Congruence with our usual work, skills and other capabilities
     2. Probability of success
     3. Fit with our current workload
     4. Our need for new contracts

In general, the outline format tends to help you identify the many specific tasks that would need to be done, whereas the flow chart tends to place the tasks into the perspectives of necessary phases and sequences. Some individuals can do the outlining men-tally, as they develop the flow charts spontaneously, but not every-one has that gift.

The Labor-Loading Chart

Still another aid to estimating is the labor-loading chart, an especially valuable tool for a service business. Figure 8.3 illustrates that by example. This device compels you to analyze how much time each principal must put into the job to get it done and then enables you to total the number of hours required of each individual. On the other hand, if you run a one-person business, instead of job titles at the heads of the columns in this chart, you can run functions that you must perform—research, writing drafts, editing your copy, revising and many other chores—and estimate the hours needed for each function.

One thing you may be sure of in estimating is this: The more detailed your analysis and planning are, the more accurate your estimate is likely to be. For one thing, the more detailed your analysis and planning, the less likely it is that you will overlook some important item, only to discover much later that you are stuck with some expense or need more time and effort than you had originally planned.

Figure 8.3 **Sample of Labor-Loading Chart**

Phase/Task	Marketing Manager	Writer	Support	Proposal Manager
Bid/No-Bid Analysis	16 hours	8 hours	4 hours	
Assign Proposal Manager	4 hours	—	—	
Select Team	8 hours	—	—	16 hours
Develop Checklist	4 hours	12 hours	4 hours	8 hours
Etc.				
TOTALS				

Chapter 9

Getting Your Price and Getting Paid

The final frontiers in business include closing sales at proper prices and collecting your bills. That, especially closing sales at the prices you have set, is as much a business skill as any other of the several skills necessary to operate a successful business. It is, in fact, a marketing skill.

Markets Are Customers, and Customers Are People

Markets are people: Customers and prospective customers. Marketing is ergo a people skill. It requires an understanding of people, both as individuals and as classes or groups. It requires an understanding of what motivates people to find something attractive or unattractive, to value it highly or not to value at all, to buy it or refuse to buy. It is an understanding of what induces people to accept and pay the prices you set or to reject and refuse to pay them. The latter objective, persuading people to accept and pay the prices you set, is itself a marketing problem. You do not market

167

your service in isolation from marketing your prices. You must market both, sometimes together, but often separately.

Depending on several circumstances, including the marketing strategy you have chosen to use and the nature of what you sell, you may be selling your service and your price together, as many marketers do. Or you may sell them separately, first the service and then the price, as other marketers do. That may come to you as a new idea, but it is a truth. You will understand that truth as we examine some examples and principles of selling—i.e., selling the service without revealing the price until you have sold the service. *Sell*, here, means *persuade*, of course: Customers must be persuaded that your price is an acceptable one, even after you have induced them to want what you sell.

Selling service and selling price require similar skills, but for many kinds of businesses and in many situations the two skills are definitely individual marketing problems. It doesn't require master selling ability to be the cheapest guy in town, but it also isn't a very profitable way to conduct a business. Of course, there are successful entrepreneurs who *appear* to be the cheapest guys in town. You may have to somehow induce customers to believe that your prices really represent the greatest economy or greatest value, although they may appear to be high, if that is your price-marketing strategy. Or your strategy may be to make what you sell somehow unique and incomparable, so price comparisons are not possible. That was reputedly the chief element of IBM's great success: Probably no competitor's service approached that of IBM. Certainly, IBM developed a reputation for outstanding service. Actually, we are talking about two marketing skills here: One is developing a successful strategy, and the other is implementing that strategy, itself a marketing skill.

It may well be a fact that you set your rates higher than those of your competitors, but you actually deliver more benefit per dollar of cost than your supposedly cheaper competitors do. Even so, it requires selling skills to put this across—to sell value, instead of price. You can't expect customers to perceive this without your help: You need to develop effective sales arguments and know how to use them with the greatest effectiveness. In marketing a certain kind of contract to government agencies, for example, I have found it possible to make myself *appear* to be the low bidder without practicing deliberate deceit, basing my strategy on the government's own system for evaluating competitive prices.

A Brief Lesson in Sales Techniques

While this is certainly not a book on marketing and sales per se, it is not possible to discuss the successful conduct of any business, much less one that aspires to get the best possible prices, without exploring the subjects of marketing and selling. (Technically, they are not the same subject, but for our purposes here we can use the terms interchangeably.)

Marketing and sales methodologies are among the subjects most widely written about, talked about, taught in colleges and lectured on from public platforms. America is a land with super-abundant consumer goods and services and is the home of marketing activities to match. Some experts in marketing say flatly that people never buy but are always sold. They are sold in print advertisements, in broadcast radio and TV commercials, in more subtle ways in movies (there are some well-paid specialists who arrange to have nationally known products mentioned and shown in feature films) and in face-to-face presentations by salespeople in your home, on the street and in the stores. American industry runs on marketing and would all but collapse without energetic, continuous and effective marketing.

Thus, it is useful and probably necessary to spend a few minutes here discussing a few of the basic principles and practices of successful selling as a foundation for getting your price, the best possible price for what you sell.

Motivation

Motivation is the key in all selling. We all act in our own interest or what we believe to be our own interest. Effective marketing therefore encourages us to find our own interest in what sellers offer and presents arguments with that objective.

We like to believe that we are reasonable, logical creatures, and we believe that we make reasonable, logical decisions. It's not so, of course. Few of us are more than marginally reasonable and logical when we care deeply about any matter. At best, our ability to be logically analytical depends on our objectivity, but we are truly objective in relatively few matters. Our political convictions are one evidence of how illogical we can be: We have actually re-elected the mayor of a large city who was, at the time, a felon in one of our prisons, as just one example. In another case, a writer who published and sold his own small book by mail found himself enjoying good sales of the book at $12.95. He knew that he still could enjoy a good profit on the book at $8.95, and so cut his price on the assumption that it would sell even more briskly at the lower price. To his dismay, he found sales declining sharply at the lower price. Obviously, the buying public did not believe that his book could be very good at the lower price. He restored the original price quickly.

The simple fact is that our emotions can and do overcome our reason and dominate our reasoning processes. Every successful marketer knows that and uses appeals to emotion as a primary sales tool.

Note how beer is sold, for example. Although some effort is made in advertising beer to try to prove it superior in some way, by far the major and most-used theme in selling beer is associating it with good times—camping out, laughing it up at the local tavern, enjoying it's cold wetness on a hot day, and in other such emotionally pleasant contexts. (Note, too, that sellers of the two major colas tend to pursue the same themes.)

Two Kinds of Motivation

There are two basic kinds of motivation: Gain and fear. Probably the most frequently used motivation is *gain motivation*, promising the customer that he or she will gain something important by buying. The fact is that this appeal works best when it "strikes a nerve"—arouses emotions sharply in persuading the customer to perceive his or her direct interest in what you promise. "How to get rich" advertisements, for example, if they are credible and convincing, can never be too long or too extravagant; the reader will devour every word and pay to get more. (Such advertisements, "long copy" in the vernacular, are often used to sell "how to succeed" and, especially, "how to get rich" books and other products.) Readers get very passionate about some subjects, such as making money, losing weight, enhancing their sex appeal and getting a more prestigious job, to name just a few of the most basic desires. They will therefore read long copy.

It's relatively easy to arouse interest by making one of those kinds of promises, promises that most of us ardently want to believe. Who doesn't want to believe that there is a lazy way to get rich, an easy way to lose weight, a shortcut to getting a better job, a secret to becoming popular with the opposite sex? If the customer believes (i.e., *feels*) strongly enough, price becomes completely secondary, rather than primary in the customer's decision. To be persuasive, however, you must follow up the promise with arguments that are credible and convincing. The word *argument*, however, does not necessarily mean logical presentation. It means anything that the customer will accept as evidence that you can and will deliver what you promise. That includes testimonials from customers, photographs, quotations from reputable sources and certifications, to name a few kinds of "proof." Physicians and lawyers usually have the walls of their offices all but wallpapered with diplomas and certificates attesting to their great skills, achievements and competence. Restaurants exhibit newspaper and magazine food columns praising their cuisine and ambience, and many eateries exhibit framed and autographed photos of celebrities who, presumably, have eaten there. Many businesses offer reproductions of or quotes from testimonials in their advertising. These are all emotional appeals, although they entail some logic also in that they are tangible evidence tending to prove the claims of excellence.

Fear Motivation and "Worry Items"

Fear motivation is probably even more powerful than gain motivation, and it is widely used. A great deal of advertising and sales copy works on the "worry item" principle. The copy anticipates what most concerns the prospect—his or her worry item—and bases the appeal on it. Many single women have the fear of being "wallflowers," for example, and many clever marketers have taken advantage of this with copy that promises them popularity and good times. That is gain motivation, but its appeal lies mostly in the worry item of being "left out of things" that many women (and probably many men, too) already have.

On the other hand, some advertising *gives* the reader a worry item and then offers the remedy, as in the well-known "ring around the collar" TV commercials or those showing spotted glassware emerging from the dishwasher if one does not use the advertised detergent. A photograph of a young father and his family—wife and small children—standing forlornly beside the smoking embers of what was their house is a powerful "headline" for an insurance advertisement. If it never occurred to the reader to have to worry about the kind of disaster suggested, that copy is likely to generate such a worry.

Some items lend themselves naturally to selling via this kind of fear motivation: Selling locks and alarms, as well as insurance, for example. But the idea can be adapted to many other kinds of items. Vitamins can be sold with copy that promises a greater sense of well-being, but the copy can also be based on warding off or preventing colds and other illnesses. Many people will find the latter idea more motivating, and none of us is completely immune to the fear of being ill. (Insecurity, to some degree, may be the sole trait we all possess in common!)

Consider, then, both negative and positive arguments—fear and gain motivation—in planning your marketing strategies and sales arguments. They are two sides of the same argument, in the end—both represent gain of a sort—but one often works far more effectively than the other. But aside from the inherent (or what appears to be inherent) advantages of one approach or the other, there is the simple matter of strategy and innovation—independent thinking and imagination. For example, the usual marketing strategy of writers of resumes is to promise that their resumes bring more job offers. But it is often effective to depart from the crowd and use a different tactic than others use. Where all of your competitors are promising resumes that bring more job offers, suppose you were to promise resumes that ensure the individual against the damage that badly written resumes may produce? That's fear motivation, but it is a perfectly valid argument. There certainly are many bad resumes written every day, and they certainly can do the individual more harm than good. Just being different, but with a reasonable sales argument, can put you out in front of all your competition and justify whatever rates you choose to ask. If your rates are to be different, something in what you offer must be different too. But the opposite linkage is the way to see this: Make what you sell somehow so different and so superior to what all your competitors offer that it is really unique. Thus your prices are immediately justified.

The "Right" Customers

Marketing or at least a major part of marketing is identifying or finding the right customers for what you wish to sell. However, you may be alone in recognizing some people as the right customers for what you sell, the people who need what you sell and stand to gain greatly from it. These customers do not always recognize themselves as people who need and can benefit from what you sell. In that case, you must educate them to see the benefit. "Education" is very much a part of the marketing process. You must educate many of your customers to the rightness of your prices for what you sell, as well as to their need for—how they will benefit from—what you sell. Here is an example of how effective customer education can be.

I wrote an article on technical writing for engineers and sent it off to the editor of an engineering professional journal, offering it for publication. The editor promptly rejected it and sent it back to me, almost by return mail, much to my mystification. I could not understand the rationale of the rejection, why he thought the piece unsuitable for his publication, as he obviously did. But I felt so strongly that it was right for his publication and ought to appear there that I was troubled by the rejection and spent some time pondering the matter. Finally, I thought perhaps I did perceive the problem. I thereupon added two sentences to introduce the first paragraph of the article and sent it back to that same editor. He accepted it as promptly as he had rejected it earlier. What magic did I work with that pair of sentences? I added the magic of education, to wit:

"Mr. Engineer, the writing you must do, technical writing, is probably the most distasteful of your duties, but it is a necessary part of your job. Here are a few tips to make that odious job just a bit easier."

My earlier failure had been my failure to recognize that a busy editor did not have time or motive to analyze my reasoning in writing that article. It was necessary for me to explain myself, to explain why his readers would benefit from my article. And when you make a claim of better quality, better product, faster service or other benefit, you must support it with some evidence, even if that is simply logical argument, as it was in this case.

Promise and Proof

Promise and proof (or "proof and promise," which I find rolls off the tongue more easily as a slogan to remind oneself of the necessary ingredients) really sum up the entire rationale of sales argument: The promise—of benefits, with most stress on one dominant benefit—is the device to demand attention and arouse interest. It is or ought to be the headline/lead in a print ad and the hook in a broadcast commercial. It should strike a nerve and make the customer want to know more. "More" is the evidence, the convincers that I label "proof." "More" is what you introduce to help you convince/persuade the customer that you can and will produce the benefit—i.e., that buying what you sell will produce that benefit.

It is essential that you provide the convincers—testimonials, logic, certifications, guarantees or whatever you have to offer for this purpose of bringing about conviction to follow interest and desire, to prove your case.

Proving Your Case

In a court of law, evidence is subject to many strict rules as to what is admissible, what weight it may be given and how it may be interpreted. In the sciences, even stricter rules are often applied to claims of discovery and other reports made by scientists. In marketing, there is only one rule of evidence: Proof is whatever the customer will accept as proof. The customer is judge and jury. If you offer what you represent to be evidence that a diet of oranges and bananas will bring about weight loss, many eager dieters will believe you because they want to believe you. But most will want some kind of proof, much as they would like to believe you. How critical or demanding the customer will be in evaluating your evidence depends to a large degree on how desperately the customer wants to believe you. Most, however, do demand something they can accept as evidence, the logical argument, at least.

Identifying Markets and Niche Markets

Success in pricing depends to some extent on the market in which you sell. Markets are customers, both individually and in classes and groups. If whatever it is that you sell is useful to a wide variety and great number of people—a resume service, for example, with a potential of millions of customers—you can choose your markets. You can address all the millions of working people as prospective customers, or you can target specific groups, such as engineers, teachers or factory workers. The choice is yours.

On the other hand, if what you sell is useful to only certain kinds of customers—renting mailing lists in small quantities, for example, with your potential limited to those selling by mail—you must find your best market. It may be small, home-based mailers or larger companies, but you will have to learn where and what your best markets are—what customers are the best market(s) for you. Or the market may be dictated to you because you can't supply large enough mailing lists to satisfy the needs of the large mailers.

Identifying your markets and learning which are your best markets is a most important element of pricing. In most cases, where you have a wide choice of possible markets, there is a wide difference among them for responsiveness to your appeals and, hence, to your ability to command good prices. One key element in getting your price lies in finding the best markets, the most receptive ones.

You may believe that you already know who is most in need of or can benefit most from what you sell, and thus you can easily identify your markets on the basis of what you already know. But you can be quite wrong. That premise can lead you to waste a great deal of time and money pursuing the wrong goals. We are all prone to making the mistake of believing that we know something to be fact when we really do not know anything of the sort. When I was busily pursuing customers for my proposal-writing services, I was certain that my best customers were bound to be small electronics manufacturing firms. My judgment was distorted by my experience. I believed that small electronics firms would be right for me because I had worked in and was familiar with that business and many people in it. I also knew that there were a great many such firms. I thought of it as an ample market, and that thought influenced my judgment by introducing some wishful thinking. I *wanted* that belief to be true.

It was only when I had wasted a great deal of time and money pursuing such prospects that I began to learn that the small computer software developers were a much better market for me. They happened to be companies who tended to feel a much greater need for what I had to sell than did electronics developers. They also tended to be smaller firms, firms of two or three people, who needed help more than many other small firms.

A Few Business Myths and Mistakes

The road to business success is often the education we get along the way. We learn much by our mistakes. It is painful, but many—perhaps most—of us learn no other way than by bitter experience that we must not assume anything to be true. We must research and test our premises before accepting them as demonstrated fact. That testing is a basic lesson of marketing. It applies here to the matter of getting your prices as much as it applies to other marketing objectives. There are many common myths in marketing, as there are in most fields. Some of these beliefs appear to be logical enough, but perhaps the logic is faulty. In any case, beware of false notions. In fact, you may recognize some of the following deceptive situations and individuals as familiar ones in your own experience.

The Ability To Pay the Price

Don't mistake the ability to pay a price with the willingness to pay it. One false notion too widely held is that all wealthy people will pay high prices unhesitatingly. Many quite wealthy people are among the world's most enthusiastic penny-pinchers. (That, in some cases, is part of the reason they have become wealthy.)

The reverse of this is equally true. Many quite ordinary people in quite ordinary financial circumstances can and will pay the top prices willingly and unquestioningly. You cannot and should not try to judge what is in the other's pocket or budget.

Making Unwarranted Judgments

Not unrelated to the ability to pay is the hazard of making judgments based on appearances. The simple fact is that wealthy people do not always dress well, live in mansions or drive Rolls-Royces. But many ordinary working people do drive expensive automobiles and dress fashionably and expensively. This is that kind of society. (The wealthy publisher, Bernarr McFadden, was notorious for appearing to be the shabbiest of vagrants and was often mistaken by those who did not know him as just that, a vagrant.)

There is another related fact. Many of us are generous or even profligate in one area of our lives and penny-pinching in another. Some will splurge on furniture and scrimp on food or drive a decrepit jalopy and dress like the Prince of Wales, for example. The individual who is most tightfisted in many respects may pay what you ask without hesitation and without question. What an individual does in one situation is not a reliable indicator of what he or she might do in a quite different situation.

You can be as easily deceived by what customers say. In some cases, they are being deliberately deceitful in the hope of persuading you—bribing you, in fact—to quote a favorable price. In other cases, they believe what they are saying, but they are still offering you false information. For example, one common gambit certain customers use as a carrot they hope will influence your price favorably is the promise of sending you lots of business.

"Oh, I've got a lot of friends who could use your service," they will assure you, beaming broadly. "I can send you lots of business if you treat me right." Or a variant: "I need a lot of this kind of work done. I can give you a lot more business if you treat me right on this little job."

My own experience tends strongly to teach me that rarely, if ever, did I get more business from those who made such promises. Where a customer gave me lots more business and/or sent me other customers, it was almost always the quiet, uncomplaining customer who paid what I asked and paid me promptly.

Aside from that, it is usually a mistake to cut your prices on the basis of any such promise as that. In fact, it is probably a mistake to cut your prices at any time or under any circumstances without a negotiation of some sort, such as we will discuss shortly. It is quite easy for customers to make vague promises of good things to happen, and there is always a great temptation to believe those promises, but caution is in order.

The Growing Need for Sales Wisdom

There seems to be a never-ending increase in costs and prices, and I have not totally ignored the subject in earlier chapters. For one, I brought up in Chapter 3 the matter of "sticker shock," a constant hazard of the times because we have had a steady inflation for many years. In some years, the prices have advanced slowly, but in other years there have been great spurts in prices, so that the price almost always came as something of a shock to the unsuspecting customer, as it did to me recently: I have worn eyeglasses almost all of my life, starting in childhood, and I recall my parents paying $5.50 for my first pair, although I know that was a bargain price, even then, and I have, of course, been paying a great deal more than that for my eyeglasses since then. Still, when I visited a branch of a chain manufacturer/retailer of eyeglasses, one that constantly advertises low prices, I experienced sticker shock of my own.

I wanted something quite simple: I wanted a pair of reading glasses, for use at the computer, to be made by taking the measure from the reading lenses of my bifocals. A great banner on the outside of the shop proclaimed all frames were available at half-price, so I entered with some confidence and advised the salesman of my needs, explaining that I wanted the most inexpensive frame available. Without hesitation, the man calmly quoted me a price of $140.

I was quite shocked. I had not paid much more than that for my bifocals, with fairly expensive frames, and I instantly rejected the offer. The clerk was speechless when I objected and did not offer to even discuss the matter, evidently uncaring whether we did business or not.

Within a few minutes I found a small shop literally around the corner where I got what I wanted for only slightly more than one-third that first quotation (for $49.95, in fact). Had the first salesperson somehow softened the blow and indicated that there was some range within which we could negotiate, we might have done business. His casual dropping of what I was sure was an excessive cost clearly implied "take it or leave it," and I left it. I will never return there, of course, although I had done business there previously. His competitor around the corner gained the customer he had lost.

Timing the Price Quotation

Can you see the lesson here? Part of the problem was the price quoted me. I certainly did not expect to have to pay that much for simple reading glasses. But much of the salesman's problem was his failure to foresee a probable problem: I had already signaled that I did not wish to spend much money by advising him that I wanted the most inexpensive frame. He made no effort at all to find out what I had in mind and probably could have sold me a relatively expensive set of eyeglasses had he explored with me something more of what I had in mind.

When I advised the proprietor of the little shop around the corner that I would use the new glasses on a limited basis and did not wish to invest much in them, he guided me to his displays of frames, pointed out the least expensive ones and invited me to browse among them to see if I could find one I liked. When I found one and took them to him to ask the price, I was already committed to some extent, emotionally, at least. I liked the frames and was ready to hear a price. (I did not expect to get away for that modest a sum, however.)

The example also shows one reason why it is wise to never volunteer a price, if it is not already part of your initial presentation, as in a price-based marketing strategy—i.e., claiming to be the cheapest guy in town. Wait to be asked, for there is little point in quoting a price for something in which the customer has not yet shown signs of great interest. However, even then do not reveal the price prematurely, before you have made a presentation and persuaded the customer to become committed to some extent, at least to the extent of becoming interested in the benefits you promise. Think of your presentation as two presentations, first of the benefits of what you sell, and then of the price.

There is a second excellent reason to delay quoting a price until you are ready to quote it: Your sales presentation is or should be based largely on the information you get from the customer. That is, it should be a dialogue, rather than a monologue, while you form an estimate of the customer's concerns—the "worry items"—and desires. Only when you believe you understand those thoroughly and have delivered your presentation in response to those, should you be ready to permit the subject to be changed and your input of useful information terminated.

And there is a third good reason for not quoting your rates prematurely: Your hourly rates may be considerably higher than those of your competitors or the market in your service area, and yet they may represent a much greater value than the nominally lower rates of competitors. (This was discussed in some depth in Chapter 2.) You need time to lay the groundwork to support this and persuade your customer to weigh and appreciate the value of what you do and sell, rather than to just look at the sticker price.

It is not difficult to delay quoting prices until you are ready to do so, especially if you are in the business of providing any kind of custom service. For example:

"Oh, yes, Mr. Greene, I will be happy to quote you a complete price, but I do need to get just a bit more information from you first."

"Right now, I could give you only a rough estimate that probably would not be accurate. If you can give me just a few more minutes, I should be able to give you an exact cost."

If you work only on an hourly rate or the project is such that an hourly rate is mandatory, you need another kind of rationale, such as this:

"Certainly I can and will quote you an hourly rate in a few minutes, but that alone won't tell you much, unless we discuss all the factors that might affect how to satisfy your need most efficiently."

"May we hold off on that for a few minutes, until I have explained just how I work. I think my rate will make a lot more sense to you then."

I have found, in practice, that it is not at all difficult to do these things. In fact, the customer's reaction to such efforts may be revealing and useful in itself in revealing clues to closing the sale on the best possible terms. That is a new phase of the sales effort: It signals the opening of negotiations.

The Matter of Negotiation

Every business transaction involves a negotiation. That word may invoke for you an image of a number of people, drawn up into opposing groups gathered around a conference table, making presentations to each other and arguing interminably over one detail after another as each party bargains with the other party for advantages, concessions and compromises.

The Meaning of Negotiation

There are, indeed, many negotiations of this description taking place every day throughout the world, but for every such formal negotiation, there are many thousands of more prosaic and undramatic exchanges taking place every day. The mere act of asking the price of some object and stating that price to an apparently interested inquirer is a negotiation in itself. And so every sale is actually the result of a successful negotiation, and every exchange that does not result in a sale is actually an unsuccessful negotiation. In short, you are negotiating with every customer or prospective customer when you discuss the sale of whatever you offer to sell. There may or may not be bargaining—a struggle to arrive at a mutually acceptable price—but there is negotiating, even if it is as simple as an inquiry of price, a statement of price and a flat acceptance or rejection.

Try to think of every sales effort as a negotiation. (The noted negotiator, Herb Cohen, author of the best-selling *You Can Negotiate Anything* [Lyle Stuart, 1980] argued that everything is negotiable.) Assume that every inquiry from someone as to your price or how you work is a sign of interest and is thus a sales opportunity. True, it might be merely an expression of idle curiosity, but you can't know that without picking up the cue and pursuing the possibility of an interested prospect and a possible sale.

Negotiation as Response to Objections

There is, of course, a substantial difference in negotiating a $50 or $100 resume-writing or word processing task and in negotiating a $25,000 or larger project. The former would normally be a spontaneous, informal negotiation—primarily questions, answers and decisions—whereas the latter might well be a formal sit-down conference lasting some appreciable time, with protracted discussions and exchanges. Negotiation does not necessarily mean that you reduce your price. Negotiation may not mean anything more than that you manage to persuade your customer to pay your price. Or you may merely review the benefits of your service or *why* your customer would be wise to close the sale with you. It may mean that you explain in greater detail what your price entails—your guarantee, follow-up service or other benefit. Perhaps your resume customer did not realize or is not taking into account that he or she gets a full dozen laser-printed copies of the resume. Or that you store the disk bearing the resume, and the customer has the right to a special price on updating or revising the resume in the future. That is, negotiation may mean more selling to answer objections, a quite normal phase of selling that is covered by every book and course on the subject of selling.

Negotiating Prices

It is commonly assumed that negotiation is concerned principally with prices and matters closely related to prices. Probably price objections are a principal precipitator of negotiating sessions. Quite commonly, a customer will like what you offer but will either object to your price or attempt to bargain with you as a matter of course. Many people believe, as Herb Cohen stated, that everything is negotiable, in the sense that they can always bargain about price.

It is probably a mistake to simply reduce your price because a customer has made it clear that you have a sale if you do so. Doing so signals an admission that your price was too high to begin with, and the customer is justified in so interpreting the cost reduction. If you are inclined to reduce your price to close the sale, whatever your reason, it is wise to make it a negotiated reduction indeed. That is, make it a compromise. Require some compensating reduction in what you will do for a reduced price.

When a customer advises you that he or she finds your price unaffordable or otherwise excessive, you can perhaps react in this way:

"I quite understand, Mrs. Customer. Let's see what we can do to get the price down a bit. Perhaps you do not need more than one printed copy of your resume? Or perhaps you won't need me to store your disk for possible future updates?"

It does not matter greatly if the reduction in service actually lowers your costs significantly. What does matter is that you have some negotiating position, some points on which you can offer compromise. Surprisingly often, the customer will demur immediately, reject any reductions in benefits and signal the end of negotiations with an acceptance of your price. Often the customer was simply routinely testing the waters to see if there was any resilience in your price. Offering a compromise, as suggested, is a far better sales practice than a flat refusal to talk about it and a firm insistence on the stated price. It supports you as a reasonable and honest businessperson in the customer's eyes.

To do this successfully, you must prepare in advance for it by structuring your service so that there are negotiable points built into it. You may, in fact, price each individually, but then they are no longer negotiating points but simply fixed prices for specific, individual services. To use them as negotiating gambits, they must be included in the package at a single price so that you can offer them up as sacrifices to reduce the price. That puts you in a commanding position if price negotiations become necessary.

Solving—and Preventing— Collection Problems

In Chapter 8 I described two omens indicating a customer who is likely to prove a reluctant payer, if not a nonpayer—i.e., a deadbeat. The individual who shows no interest at all in your price, never even mentioning the subject, suggests by this omission that he or she is one of those who will not pay your bill. The individual who assures you blandly that price is no object is also suggesting that possibility that it is no object because he or she has no intention of paying it! It is unnatural for anyone, and especially so for someone who is also a business owner or executive, to disavow an interest in costs. It is ample reason in itself for suspicion. Certainly, meeting such a prospective customer is not reason for rejoicing, as it might seem to someone inexperienced in meeting and doing business with such customers. It should invoke your alarm system.

Retainers and Deposits Help

Aside from this, the problem of collecting for your work is a real one in many situations. Even when you run a small business on a strictly cash basis, you can't avoid having collection problems at least occasionally. When I wrote resumes on a cash basis, occasionally a customer came in, collected the resume and then, while I handed over an invoice, expecting payment, blandly promised to send me a check.

What are you to do under those circumstances? Can you snatch back the resume or brochure by force? Of course not. It is illegal to do so, as well as impracticable. Once you have surrendered physical possession of the product, you may have a claim against it, but you cannot legally seize it without a court order. (Or so legal counsel informed me a long time ago.)

Any business that does custom work ought to require a substantial payment in advance. Usually, in such a business, the work and the product that results is of no use to anyone but the individual customer. Certainly, it is worthless to you. If the customer never picks the product up, you are stuck completely. You must therefore protect yourself with enough of the bill paid in advance to cover your costs at least. But there is yet another reason for requiring retainers or advance deposits: It helps ensure payment in general. Thus you do not even start the job without a substantial deposit. (Note that advance payments also are a great aid to solving cash flow problems, although that is a side benefit and not the primary purpose in requiring deposits and retainers.)

For small jobs, such as resume writing, I would suggest one-half in advance, reducing the possible risk by one-half immediately. Actually, it reduces risk by much more than one-half. The customer who pays you a proper deposit is rarely the customer who gives you any problem over the remainder of the bill. (I have had my share of uncollectible bills and bills I had to pay large collection fees on or settle for much less than the full amount. Only once, however, have I lost anything on a bill where I had the advance retainer. Even then my loss was a small one, as I collected less than the full balance remaining at completion of the job.)

Conversely, the customer who can't or won't pay you a proper deposit should invoke your alarm system immediately: That is a customer who is far more likely to give you a problem collecting any of your fee. Or so my experience indicates.

With all small custom projects you should make the terms one-half in advance and the remainder on completion, and make your policy clearly understood. If you have customers visiting you at your office, it's a good idea to post signs that announce this policy quite clearly. Whether you receive customers directly or do business by mail, as many small businesses do, your policy ought to be clearly stated in your literature—sales letters, brochures and other such materials.

The same policy is a wise one for larger projects, although for the more protracted project the proportions may be different. I know of some consultants who ask for one-half of their estimated fee up front as a retainer even on large projects, although I have always thought that one-third was ample, with another one-third paid at some defined midpoint, and the final one-third paid on completion. The principles are the same, however: The customer who pays you the retainer you ask for rarely gives you problems of payment later, and the customer who cannot or will not pay your retainer is one to beware of.

The Need for Binding Authorizations

There are cases where pursuing this policy poses problems. For example, the large corporation may well be so bureaucratic that it requires a ton of paperwork and two or three weeks of time to generate a check as a retainer. Where the project must be started immediately, you are faced with the problem of starting work without your usual retainer. Here, you must use some judgment. If the customer is a well-established and sizable corporation whose ability to pay is unquestionable, it is safe to proceed if you have binding authorization. That is a most important consideration.

By "binding authorization," I mean something in writing that commits the customer formally to pay you whatever is the stated sum for your work. Normally, that is a contract or a purchase order, stipulating the work and price, and signed by a suitable company official. (The purchase order is really a contract, too, but a rather informal one, generally issued in circumstances that do not require negotiation of a formal contract.) As an alternative, used in some cases (often where immediate service is needed, and even a purchase order takes considerable time to generate), a company official may issue a letter of agreement or a letter of authorization that serves the same purpose as a contract. Or a letter may be issued to authorize start of the work while a formal contract is being negotiated and agreed to.

Why this need for something in writing? Is there some danger that a prestigious, large corporation intends to defraud you? Of course not; that is not the problem at all. The problem is that some individual will give you a verbal commitment without having the authority to bind his company in that manner. The company's comptroller is certainly not going to pay you without something on paper to authorize the disbursement.

This kind of thing—i.e., unauthorized orders by someone in the company who lacks proper authority—can happen in business organizations of any kind and any size, even in government agencies. Where it is especially likely to happen is in the case of a change: Typically, as a project proceeds, it becomes apparent that more is needed than was originally contracted for, and the client issues a verbal authorization to do additional work. Unless you have some written authorization amending the original purchase order or contract, you run the serious risk of never being paid for the extra service.

The Special Problem of "Changes"

One difficult collection problem can arise from the requirement to make changes to the project originally undertaken and contracted for as a fixed-price job. Either the project proved to require more than you estimated—perhaps because the customer did not reveal to you all the facts you should have known or perhaps the customer demanded additional work as he or she saw the work progress and had new ideas about what he or she wanted. You feel entirely justified in asking for more money than you originally quoted, and the customer feels entirely justified in refusing to pay more. The real core of the dispute revolves around what you agreed to—what your contract means.

The tendency to quote an hourly rate because of the common difficulty of estimating the labor and other costs of an impending project has been noted or referred to more than once in the preceding pages. Despite this difficulty, customers do often require a firm, fixed-price bid or quotation or a ceiling on labor hours to be specified and contracted for.

The principal problem in satisfying that customer requirement is often the vague nature of the customer's description of what is required—i.e, the lack of a firm, well-detailed specification of the work and/or the end product required. It is not an unusual problem at all. It is quite commonly the case that a customer knows what the problem is and what he or she wants in general or qualitative terms but not in specific or quantitative terms. Under those circumstances, you see an unacceptable risk involved in guaranteeing the result called for at some fixed price.

There are two possibilities here:

1. In many cases, you are much more expert and experienced in whatever is normally required for such a problem as that stated, and you are confident that you can furnish a specification and therefore quote a guaranteed fixed price.

2. You believe that you know what needs to be done and can quantify the work to be done, but you are not highly confident of it and thus see considerable risk in pricing it at a fixed price.

Either way, you can handle the problem by writing that specification and contracting for it. That is, your specification becomes part of the contract. (If you have submitted your specification as part of your proposal, make sure that your proposal is included in the contract either directly or by reference.)

The point is that when the customer agrees to your specification and contracts on that basis, you are protected against overruns due to the specification falling short or the customer deciding to demand more from you than was specified in your contract. (That kind of demand, known as a "change," is not unusual.)

Remember that the specification must be detailed, especially in a quantitative sense—numbers of hours, pages, illustrations, lines of code or whatever units are appropriate. It must be highly specific, even if you are not absolutely certain that it will be sufficient. It must advise your customer *how much* of your services the quoted dollars will buy. (Presumably, you are experienced enough to make the accuracy of your estimate highly probable.)

There are sometimes cases where you can see more than one possible appropriate specification because the customer has been unclear. A wise way to propose in this case is to offer alternatives: The least costly way to get a minimally satisfactory result and one or more alternative ways to get higher quality or in some way superior results. (I have done this in offering an end product, a manual of different qualities, for example.) This often produces a much better price than you might have realized had you not offered the most modest price and explained the attractive alternatives possible.

In any case, you are protected only if there can be no question as to what the contract calls for. Writing a clear specification into the contract thus protects you. However, it does not protect you against the customer's casual and informal requests for work not covered in the contract. All too often the customer—and that may mean someone representing the customer, perhaps a low-level employee—asks you, verbally, for services not covered in your contract. You demur and are assured that you will be paid extra for that extra work.

There is a serious risk here. That individual may or may not have the authority to guarantee payment, but you are totally unprotected without that binding authorization referred to earlier: You should require something formal in writing, acknowledging the legality of the request and guaranteeing payment, either as a contract amendment or as a separate order.

This and the other measures recommended here solve collection problems by preventing collections from becoming problems.

A Problem of Bureaucratic Crawl

There is also the occasional problem of having your bill tied up in a bureaucratic maze, and large corporations can become dismayingly bureaucratic. Even in the normal course of events, many large corporations take longer to pay their bills than government agencies do, as I found out when I waited as long as 90 days to collect from some quite large and prominent clients. In one case, where the U.S. Postal Service owed me a considerable sum, even the contracting officer couldn't help me. It took weeks of calls to learn, finally, that the payment-approval procedure was slightly more complex than with most government agencies—it required an extra signature. Until I took steps to get that signature I could not get paid.

I learned from that experience to always ascertain what the payment process is when I do work for large organizations. Distressingly often, the individuals who authorize projects are completely at sea when it comes to payment procedures.

I found, too, that bureaucracy can produce other problems of payment. I discovered that when a client took excessively long to pay me, the problem was often that the first individual who had to approve your invoice—i.e., certify that the work was done and payment should be made—still had my invoice in his in-basket and had not gotten around to signing it. I found it helpful to walk my invoice through myself, especially on large projects for large organizations, by personally delivering my invoice to the client and asking him to sign it so I could drop it off at the comptroller's office. (I found that government agencies could pay even more promptly than corporations when I did this.)

Chapter 10

Setting Prices
To Work for
Government Agencies

The bad news about doing business with government agencies is that you have to endure and be prepared to combat bureaucratic apathy and foot-dragging sometimes. The good news is that it is a big, big market, you can make good profits there and you can be sure of getting paid, usually promptly, if you learn and follow the rules.

It's the Biggest Market/Set of Markets in the World

Even with the spending cutbacks of federal, state and local governments in recent years, the total cost of all government procurement is staggering: It runs to hundreds of billions of dollars every year. The federal government alone spends well over $200 billion annually, with more than $60 billion in off-budget items, such as that of the U.S. Postal Service. Small business gets its share: At least $65 billion from federal agencies and probably about three times that from the many thousands of state and local government

193

agencies. There are nearly 22,000 state, county and municipal governments, each with numerous agencies and departments (the federal government alone operates in nearly 40,000 offices and other locations). There are also more than 41,000 local school districts and special districts, each of which has its own purchasing power. When you look at these figures, it is easy to understand why sales opportunities in these markets reach hundreds of billions of dollars each year.

With markets of that magnitude, and with competitiveness being as keen and aggressive as it is, one can only wonder why so many businesses, small and large, tend to ignore and neglect governments as markets: In fact, a surprisingly small fraction of all American companies are serious and consistent contenders for government contracts.

As nearly as it is possible to analyze this paradox, the apparent disinterest in pursuing government business is due to at least two factors: One is that many marketers are discouraged from trying to win government contracts because they do not understand government procurement, and another is that many do not know how to even begin to research sales opportunities in government markets. Government markets are strange and alien territory to marketers, and they are apparently fearful of venturing there.

Reluctance to pursue government business is also due in some part to the many myths about doing business with the government: The allegedly impenetrable forest of red tape, the belief in interminable delays in getting paid and the numerous supposed difficulties in general of dealing with bureaucrats (as though our supercorporations are any less bureaucratic). These beliefs tend to discourage marketing directors of even the largest corporations. Small business owners are often discouraged because they think that they are "not big enough to handle government contracts." On one occasion, I joined a company as a branch manager. The company was grossing about $8 million in annual sales at the time. When, not long after joining them, I won the company's first government contract, the president of the company was astonished. He did not realize that government agencies make many small purchases ("small" in government terms, that is), as well as many large ones.

Pricing projects for government agencies while still being competitive has never been easy. In at least some ways, pricing bids for contracts tends to call more for guesstimates than methodical or logical estimates. Despite the current government emphasis on buying more commercial products and services at standard market prices and simplifying government procurement in general, government requirements are often highly specialized and require custom work. However, through experience I have learned some principles and rules of thumb that help greatly to apply at least some reason and method to the pricing of government projects.

Assessing Difficulty Level and Time Requirements

I find it important to evaluate a prospective government project quite carefully before offering a bid or proposal. One practice I have found helpful in trying to set a price on a prospective government contract is getting a fix on the difficulty level, especially on the amount of time that will be required to do the job. One important measure of difficulty, in terms of probable time required, is determining in advance who will be reviewing and approving the work done or the end product delivered. The names or functions of the reviewers are not matters of concern. It is getting some realistic idea of how many reviewers are involved and how many signatures are necessary to get the work accepted and the invoice approved for payment, as I related in Chapter 8. That is an important consideration because it is a good indicator of how many meetings and discussions you are likely to be asked to attend, how many revisions to your original work are likely to be demanded, as well as how long you may have to wait to get final approval and get paid. Thus, where there is a stated requirement or even a good indication of a large number of reviews and approvals, it is wise to set your price high enough to compensate you for this and to feel no regrets if the customer finds your price too high to pay. You would probably have regretted accepting the contract at a lower price.

On one occasion I told the government executive for whom I was quoting a price that my price was based in part on that consideration of meetings and delays. He quite agreed that I was justified in anticipating such difficulties and agreed readily then to my price. (I have often found that simple honesty can be a powerful sales tool.)

In general, relative to that consideration, I have usually found the small task to be much more profitable than the large project. Usually, the small task is undertaken to satisfy the need of a single individual or, at least, a single individual is responsible for the task and will make all decisions regarding it. In one case, for example, I was awarded a purchase order to develop a rough draft into a small brochure for the Public Buildings Service. When I turned my copy in, the in-house editor complained that he disagreed with how I had divided words that were hyphenated and refused to approve my invoice for payment. (It was irrelevant how I divided the words in my manuscript because the agency was going to send the manuscript to the Government Printing Office to be typeset and printed. The GPO would divide the words as they saw fit, but this bureaucrat was a classic example of bureaucratic obstinacy.) I explained the problem to his superior, who had given me the job; he agreed with me and approved my invoice himself, quickly settling the problem. On many occasions, when my invoice was not paid as promptly as I knew it should have been, the problem was, as usually, bureaucratic sloth: My invoice had become a more or less permanent resident of someone's in-basket and would have been there permanently had I not taken action. I was usually able to settle such problems by telephone.

Those kinds of minor bureaucratic difficulties are usually resolved as simply as this with the small jobs. Not so with the larger ones. They usually involve a number of people, and they can quite easily turn into protracted negotiations and much wasted time.

In general, with the small jobs, there is also much less haggling and negotiating about prices, and there is far less marketing cost—overhead, remember—in pursuing the small jobs. In fact, in many cases, when you have developed a friendly relationship with the agency's personnel, they come to you with their needs, just as commercial customers do: Since the requirements for competition on such jobs is negligible (especially those under $2,500 in the federal procurement system), government executives who like your work will often become more or less steady sources of small jobs. That makes marketing to governments for those small jobs much more like marketing to the private sector than is the case in marketing the larger projects, where the project is highly visible and competition is quite sharp and intensive.

Overall, in addition to being an easier and less costly marketing problem, you almost always have the best chance to get top dollar for your services and product when bidding and winning the small projects.

Getting Special Information about Prices

One advantage of contracting with government agencies is that they are spending public money—your money and mine—and so must make information public in general, and especially under the Freedom of Information Act. To take advantage of that, ask whether the impending contract is for services under a new and original contract—one of its kind and never done before—or renewal of an existing contract. Most government contracts are for one, two or three years, and many are contracts the agency maintains permanently but must rebid competitively each time it has run its term and is about to expire. If the contract is one of that type, there is, of course, a history of what it has cost the government in years past. Under the Freedom of Information Act, you have the right to be told what the agency has paid under the contract in prior years. That gives you a good idea of the proper rates to consider in formulating your bid.

Where there is a laundry list of services for a "task order" kind of agreement, it is not easy to make cost comparisons among bidders. Consider this, for example, as a comparison of hourly rates bid by four bidders for an assorted set of services:

Service	Bidder A	Bidder B	Bidder C	Bidder D
Writing	$38	$42	$32	$48
Editing	31	28	38	29
Word Processing	24	29	21	22
Illustrating	26	27	41	40

Using the Special Information: Pricing Strategies

Unless you can set a definite quantity of hours for each service, there is no absolute way to determine who is the low bidder here. This type of contract calls for standardized rates, however, expressly because the customer does not know how much of each service will be required over the duration of the contract. (Such contracts are often referred to as "indefinite quantity contracts.") The general method used to decide who is the low bidder is to make up a bench test: Make up a hypothetical task that would require a given quantity of each service, and price the job as it would be billed by each of the bidders.

It is important to know what the government has been paying for each kind of service. It is also important, in many ways even more important, to know how much of each kind of service the agency has been buying. If there is one service of which they have bought little or none in the past, for whatever reason, you have an immediate opportunity to appear to be the lowest bidder without cutting your prices. You offer that service at a throwaway price. That brings down the average of your service costs (as determined in a bench test) quite a bit without costing you much of anything. The risk is small; the gain is great. You gain a great cost advantage.

This is a general strategy that can be and is used in other situations by resourceful veterans of government contracting. It is, again, a matter of shaping customers' perceptions. "Low bid" is not always a literal fact. There is such a thing as *appearing* to be a low bidder when it is difficult to ascertain in an absolute sense who is a low bidder.

State and Local Procurement Systems

State governments and many county and municipal governments have surprisingly large and diverse needs, rivaling those of the federal government, except for major military equipment. The state of California, in fact, lists supply groups and items within the groups almost as numerous and diverse as those of the federal government.

In general, state and local governments each have a centralized purchasing and supply organization in the state capitals, county seats and city/town halls. Small communities are likely to have a single officer of purchasing and supply, and that may even be another hat for some official with other duties. In the larger government organizations, the procurement department will have a number of buyers, each assigned some specific area—e.g., computer hardware and software, office supplies, engineering services and others, according to the needs. Annual supply or indefinite quantity contracts are quite commonly awarded, with the purchasing agency also a supply department.

Some purchasing authority may be allocated to some of the departments, although the usual practice is to have the department make a request of the central supply organization to arrange to have the service or goods contracted for. Still, even then, you may have to sell your service to the department directly, after which the central supply will make arrangements to buy from you.

Most of the states and larger municipalities have public literature available to you on request, explaining their systems and needs. Usually, there is a registration form you must file, which may act also as a request to have your name placed on the bidder's list. You may write to the organization for literature, but all of them urge personal visits by vendors as the most effective way of initiating business relationships and selling to the purchasing groups.

Most states and many municipalities also have special programs and services for small businesses and minority-owned businesses. These include loan programs, set-aside and preference programs (especially for businesses within the state or municipality), counseling and other helpful services. Today, some of these are made available online via the Internet. (See the Appendix for relevant information.)

The Federal Procurement System

In the federal system, procurement is highly decentralized, as well as highly diversified, with all major agencies (and all their branch offices, in many cases) having their own contracting officers and power to make most of their purchases independently. There are, in fact, some 125,000 contracting officers in the federal system, which gives you some idea of the number of purchasing offices. However, there is also the government's own "general store," in the existence of the Federal Supply Service (FSS), a branch of the General Services Administration (GSA), which buys and stocks many commodities that the agencies may buy from them. But it does not stop there, either: The FSS also awards hundreds of annual supply contracts for a wide variety of goods and services that any agency may order from the supplier under the FSS contract with that supplier. (These contracts are informally referred to as the "Federal Supply Schedules.")

These purchasing facilities of the Federal Supply Service are made available to many state and local government agencies, and even to some major government contractors under the terms of their contracts. So your market is not necessarily the federal government alone when you do business with and through the FSS.

In general terms, there are two seminal ideas behind all public procurement—purchases made with public (taxpayer's) money—in a democratic government such as ours. One is to afford everyone an equal opportunity to compete for and participate in the system as a supplier. As citizens with equal rights and equal standing, we are presumably equally entitled to compete for and win government contracts.

The other reason for the principle of mandatory competition is to provide the government all the advantages of competition in procurement, including maximum number of options and ideas and honest pricing. But this concept has two aspects to it, the benefits of price and the benefits of quality or value. That requires a bit of discussion because minimum prices too often may mean minimum—unacceptable—quality. (One would be understandably reluctant to rely on a parachute supplied by the low bidder.) Still, competition in procurement applies to pricing, of course, and is most frequently thought of in that connection.

Normally, competition drives prices down and thus compels suppliers to be maximally efficient, and that is a general benefit. Government buyers presumably desire to get the most for our money just as any of us do when buying as private individuals. Competition, therefore, while it applies solely to costs, in some cases, applies more significantly to other factors in other cases, in cases where quality is a prime consideration and low bids are likely to mean low quality.

Aside from the aforementioned considerations, there are some hard and firm facts about costs and pricing government contracts that you may rely on. For example, you should understand in advance the basic rules and requirements of the several types of procurements, and other factors affecting them. Following is some basic information you need to know, if you are to price these kinds of requirements effectively.

Types of Procurement and Contracts

There are several general types of government contracts and government methods of procurement, an inevitable result of the complexities of modern-day society and the resultant complex needs of government. The Department of Defense, with its subset of military departments, is certainly a major element that consumes a major portion of our procurement dollars even today, in the post–Cold War era with reduced needs for military readiness. Over the years, a number of sets of procurement regulations and numerous memoranda and other ancillary documents grew up. In more recent years, these have been combined into one set of Federal Acquisition Regulations, referred to commonly as the FAR. Still, that has not changed the basic nature and philosophies of government procurement, especially as standardized under a uniform procurement code developed by a special committee of the American Bar Association. This code is followed by most state and local governments, as well as by the federal system, with this exception, already noted above: In the case of state and local governments, purchasing and supply tends to be centralized, unlike federal procurement, the authority of which is broadly decentralized. Despite that quite significant difference, buying methods and philosophies tend to be quite similar in kind, if not in degree. The federal Small Purchases Act, for example, defines small purchases as those under $25,000, whereas most state and local governments define small purchases as less than $10,000, $2,500 or even $500.

Sealed Bids

Sealed bids, known as "IFB" (Information for Bid and Award) in the federal system, are strictly price competitions, with awards going to the lowest bidder in each case. The bad news is that when you sign and submit a sealed bid to a government agency, you are committed and can be held to your quoted price (although you probably will not be so held). The good news is that the contract is unquestionably yours when you are the low bidder.

This means that you must be quite careful in estimating and pricing. If you have been overly optimistic or for any other reason have underpriced the job, there is no recourse: The government can require that you do the job at the stated price. If the error is a gross and obvious one, the government is likely to permit you to withdraw your bid—may even suggest that you do so—but there is no guarantee of that.

Negotiated Procurement

Contracts awarded as the result of calling for and reviewing competitive proposals are negotiated awards, in which being the low bidder may or may not be decisive or even helpful because a selection committee will make the evaluation and judgment as to which of the proposals submitted best serves the agency's needs. In fact, bidding too low in this type of procurement may hurt your chances because it may be interpreted as evidence that you do not understand the agency's requirement and thus will be unable to deliver what you promise. Writing a proposal that gives you a margin of profit at minimal risk is probably much more art than science, and producing a winning proposal is probably much more a matter of marketing wisdom and resourcefulness than of literary skills, important though the latter are.

Negotiated procurements are so called because price is not necessarily the determining factor, the proposal does not necessarily commit you and the government is free to call on you to negotiate the terms of the contract, including the price. That may be a formal session around a conference table, or it may be an informal one via telephone or letter, depending most on the size of the contract. The negotiation may call for your best and final offer, giving a chance to review your prices and to see if you are willing to reduce them, or it may be simply a request that you confirm your offer (a proposal is an offer, not a bid, and is not legally binding in the sense that a signed bid is binding). It may concern price only, or it may concern items of performance. Or there may be no further communication, but merely an announcement that you are awarded the contract or even the mere arrival of the contract in the mail. Usually, you will be asked to confirm that your offer stands, since you already signed the contract when you completed the official form, and all that is necessary to execute the contract and put it in force is for the appropriate government official (usually the contracting officer) to sign it also.

Small Purchases

All governments make special provisions for small purchases, simplifying the processes and paperwork required. The federal government currently sets small purchase limits much higher than do state and local governments, as noted earlier, although the intent and general philosophy are the same. They do not wish to enter into a great deal of paperwork to contract for small jobs.

Generally speaking, the entire procurement process is greatly simplified when the procurement is classed as a small purchase. Competition under small purchase provisions is informal and may be bypassed completely for the purchases near the lower levels of cost. Small purchases may be made by formal contracts but are usually made by purchase order, a much simplified contracting procedure. In the federal procurement system, small purchase procurement practices are broken down further, by how much even informal competition is required and by the size of the purchase. At the same time, the Small Purchase Act does not compel the contracting official to turn to purchase orders and other simplified procurement procedure but merely permits it; the contracting officer may opt for formal contracting even for contracts well under the $25,000 ceiling.

Quotations

As a preliminary to issuing a contract or even an invitation to bid or propose, an agency may issue an RFQ or Request for Quotations. Presumably, the agency will then accept the lowest quotation and issue that quoter a purchase order, which is the scenario contemplated as the rationale for issuing an RFQ. However, there are exceptions to this, and I have known some agencies to use RFQs as RFPs to request proposals for relatively simple projects.

Selected Source Procurement

It is possible even in the case of large contracts to exempt them from the normal requirements for competition in procurement, and it is done so more or less regularly under a number of justifications: The law permits and authorizes exceptions for exceptional circumstances where it is clearly in the interest of the government to select a contractor with whom to negotiate without permitting others to compete. (Usually, that contractor has some unique qualification for the project.) That ought not to concern us, normally, for it applies to relatively rare cases of usually highly technological work. It is helpful, however, to be aware that such circumstances sometimes exist so you can understand the public procurement systems, although this aspect does not usually affect you directly or indirectly.

What Governments Buy

Governments generally, and the federal government in particular, buy almost every kind of goods and services imaginable, even some that are rarely purchased by anyone buying in or for the private sector. Many government procurements are highly specialized and rarely called for by anyone in the private sector, but some requirements go even beyond this and are truly unusual or novel. The federal government, for example, has awarded contracts for such unusual services as these:

- Rental of mules, with handlers
- Sale of prophylactics on the streets of Pakistani cities
- Theatrical presentations in national historical buildings
- Go-go dancers to perform in military service clubs
- Rounding up of wild horses and burros in the western wilderness areas

For this reason, a large part of success in doing business with the government lies in the ability and willingness to respond to unusual requests and to tailor services to government's special needs. These are often services that must be performed on-site—on government premises—either because they call for skills and experience not available except in the private sector or they require more manpower than the government can provide. A great many government facilities are actually operated by a private contractor. Many government-owned mainframe computer systems, for example, have long been run by private contractors. The Postal Service launched a correspondence-course system for its employees and awarded a contract for its operation. And the trend toward "privatization," a new term to designate such turning over of operations to contractors, is more and more an objective for cost-cutting to reduce the national debt and annual deficits.

Project Budgets and Other Considerations

To bid successfully and at the right prices for government contracts, you need to understand the government procurement systems, with their legal controls and requirements. How the government buys—statutes and regulations governing procurement systems and methods—is not exactly the same subject as how to sell to the government, but you do need to understand it. For one, to respond most effectively to the an invitation to bid or, especially to propose, it helps a great deal if you understand the reasons for the government turning to the private sector for help. Do they, for example, need a contractor's specialized skills and knowledge to do something for which they lack the capability, or are they simply shorthanded and need more "hands and feet"? The answer to that certainly influences how you respond and what you think is a proper price.

The nature of your competition for the work is another consideration. How much competition do you have?

One thing you should understand is that the agency has a budget established for the contract, representing their estimates of what the contract ought to cost. That budget may be the best estimate that can be made by agency personnel, or it may be a figure developed as a result of issuing an RFQ to gather figures. Estimating what that budget is helps you also.

Budget-Connected Risks

The budget is always a factor, an important one to both the customer and the supplier—you. Normally, the budget is a ceiling on the job: It is the amount of money available for the contract. Only bids or proposals priced within the bounds of the budget can be considered, unless the price exceeds the budget only to the extent that bargaining it down to the budget level appears to be feasible. Thus, a bid that is far in excess of the government's budget is likely to result in immediate disqualification of that proposal. On the other hand, it sometimes happens that the customer has completely underestimated what the project is likely to cost and therefore all proposals ask for prices far in excess of the budget that was established. That necessarily results in one of several possible courses of action:

- The project budget can be enlarged to meet the cost estimates, if funds are available and the project is considered to be important enough to justify a greater cost.

- The statement of work may be amended and the proposers invited to revise their proposals and cost efforts accordingly. Or, if there are only a few proposals deemed acceptable technically, each proposer may be invited to a negotiation at which the requirement will be scaled back and new cost estimates requested accordingly. This would include asking each proposer to submit an amendment to his or her original proposal.

- The project may be canceled and reconfigured for a new procurement effort immediately, or it may be deferred to next year's procurements.

- The project may be dropped entirely as not important enough to merit further effort.

There is thus always the risk that the government has underestimated by a wide margin how much they must budget to finance a project, as noted, and therefore no contract will be awarded, regardless of the quality of the proposals submitted. That is a risk. In fact, quite often the agency will state plainly in the descriptive matter (as part of the package of paper known colloquially as the "bid set") that funds are not yet available. That means the agency will be able to fund the contract if their budget is everything they expect. But if Congress does not give them all the money they have asked for, or if the top management of their agency does not distribute the funds as planned, the project may never be funded. I had the experience several times of "winning" proposal competitions for contracts that were never awarded because they were never funded. Some contractors will not respond to requests for bids or proposals where such a notice is given and may even inquire as to whether funds are already available before deciding whether to respond or not.

Pursuing Relevant Marketing Intelligence

To get the right price, you must be able to estimate the agency's probable budget with some degree of accuracy. In fact, it appears to me, it is rash to proceed with a bid or proposal without having some estimate of the customer's budget. The risk of losing a bid because your price is too high has its flip side: It is possible to lose because your price is too low! If your price is too far under the agency's budget for the procurement, the evaluators of your proposal may interpret that as your failure to understand the requirements or to your lack of appropriate experience.

Ordinarily, you might assume that the budget for any stated procurement could be estimated by the description of the work included in the bid set, the Statement of Work or SOW, as it is commonly referred to. But that assumes the agency understands the work and the market prices well enough to have estimated the cost accurately in establishing a budget, an assumption not often warranted. Quite often the agency's budget has little relation to the needs as described or as they appear to you to be described. That is, all too often, the SOW is not specific enough to be a guide. But it may only *appear* to be not specific enough to be a guide.

That can be because the agency's writer of the SOW is not a very skilled writer, is not too familiar with the work or is deliberately leaving broad gaps to encourage imaginative and innovative responses. In all these cases, if you somehow reach an estimate of the budget but conclude that the budget is not enough to buy what the SOW indicates the agency wants, you may decide that the best thing to do is to propose a program that is reasonably responsive within the limits of what the budget will buy. But if you are unable to make even an estimate of the probable budget, there is another approach possible, which we shall get to here.

Finding Clues to Pricing

Occasionally, a Statement of Work will state plainly the amount of money that the agency has available for the project. That is a rare exception, although I have known it to happen. Most contracting officials are likely to protest vigorously telling bidders what prices they ought to submit. On the other hand, many times the bid set includes clear clues to the amount of the in-house budget.

One clue that I have seen often in work statements is the government's estimate of the amount of labor required. A work statement may, for example, include an estimate that 1,000 hours or one-half a person-year of professional time will be required for some task. That is, of course, a clear guide to the budget. If you wish to make a rather general estimate, you may consider that a professional person-year, with suitable clerical support and overhead, must be billed out at some approximate figure that would be typical for that position. You might, for example, thus start with a rough estimate of perhaps $45,000. Or you might start with the direct labor cost of the professional and calculate probable support requirements in some form of labor-loading chart. (An example of such a chart appeared as Figure 8.3.)

The advantage of using such a chart is that it is a specific planning tool. It makes you base your estimate much more on hard planning than on seat-of-the-pants or "gut feeling" guesstimates, as discussed in Chapter 8. In any case, work statements often include clues to the agency's own estimate of cost and established budget for the procurement. Here are other examples:

One RFP called for supplying on-site cataloging services at a NASA center. The required service was quantified in terms of the amount of cataloging work to be performed, not in terms of how many people were to be employed. This was one of those permanent functions always contracted for, and it was time to permit competition, as required by law, for the contract. The billing would be for the full-time service of some number of individuals to perform the services, so the device of quantifying the work in terms of cataloging volume, rather than identifying the number of people and their qualifications was an obvious effort to make it difficult to bid and to make it easy to maintain the current staff and its management.

Normally, a contender for such a contract has the right to visit the site and examine it. Typically, the incumbent contractor will "hide" personnel and otherwise make it as difficult as possible for a new contender to gather useful information. This was the case here: The incumbent contractor managed to find an excuse every day to postpone our visit to the site, as the bid deadline approached.

An intensive study of the SOW finally produced the information. Buried in the lengthy, solid blocks of text were identifications of the staff by title—Chief Cataloger, Assistant Cataloger and Clerk/Secretary. With that knowledge in hand, it was possible to prepare and submit a winning bid for the contract.

In another case, where the contract would call for a laundry list of services, it was at first difficult to find a way to be competitive with the prices currently being paid, which I learned by filing a suitable request under the Freedom of Information Act. Again, intensive study of the RFP revealed among routine supporting documents a special, small section that provide a number of definitions and explanations of the terms used in the SOW. Some of them were shockers. For example, a "page" of typing was defined in such manner—so many lines, double-spaced and with line measures—that it was revealed to approximate not more than one-half the amount of copy we would normally consider to be a page. That, with our list of prices currently being paid, made it easy enough to be competitive in prices for typing, editing and proofreading.

I have found it almost always possible to uncover such clues, reading between the lines of the SOW and other sections of the

RFP, or otherwise ferreting out key information. It requires reading and rereading the RFP because many of the clues are not revealed to you as such until you know just what you are looking for.

Presenting Your Cost Figures

Many people are thoroughly frustrated by bureaucratic practices, for they often do pose problems, perhaps not quite Kafkaesque, but still infuriatingly irrational. That is the negative view of bureaucracy. The positive view is that the irrationality of bureaucracy can often be employed to advantage. You might not think that semantics or rhetoric would play a large part in pricing for maximum results, perhaps, but that would be underestimating what you can do when dealing with a bureaucracy. Here is an example:

The U.S. Department of Commerce includes a Minority Business Development Agency that was once called the Office of Minority Business Enterprise, known familiarly by its acronym OMBE. An executive of a regional office of OMBE approached me one day to ask if I would be interested in presenting a half-day seminar in government contracting to a small group in nearby Wilmington, Delaware. I agreed and, at the request of the agency, submitted my letter proposal, asking for a fee of $300 and travel expense. It was promptly approved, and I traveled to Wilmington a few days later and delivered the seminar. I was subsequently paid, of course, with a check from the Treasury Department.

Not long after, someone from the headquarters OMBE office in Washington called and, referring to the seminar I had delivered in Wilmington, asked if I would deliver a similar seminar to the headquarters staff at a Washington hotel where a meeting was to be held. I agreed and submitted a letter proposal similar to that which I had earlier submitted to the Region III office of OMBE.

That resulted in a telephone call from OMBE. The caller expressed his regrets that the office could not approve my budget of $300. Their maximum daily fee for a consultant, I was told, was $150. They could approve that, even though I was asked for only a half-day of my time, but they could not pay me $300 for that half-day.

I responded that I would submit an amended letter proposal, so that they could disregard the original one.

My amended proposal divided my fee into two parts:

Preparation to deliver seminar: $150
Delivery of seminar: 150
Total Fee: $300

The amended proposal was accepted without a murmur.

One should always try to avoid the use of the very word *consultant* when bidding to government agencies. I do not know what the agencies think a proper daily fee for a consultant is today, but it has always been far below the realities of the marketplace for consultants.

One lesson of this experience is, of course, to be careful in the language chosen, but there is a deeper level of meaning here. It is generally a good tactic to help a customer *understand* your prices. In the case cited here, I had blithely assumed that the customer would know that one does not deliver a seminar on the spur of the moment, without preparation. But the customer did not understand that.

Many people do not compete for government contracts because they refuse to reveal the details of their overhead and other business costs. Government contracts do not always call for such detailed revelation, but often they do. It can be advantageous in those cases to be able to report a modest overhead figure, since many contracting officials tend to judge the efficiency of suppliers by their overhead rates. However, there is a distinct effort today to increase government buying in commercial channels, and that may work some changes in the nature of much of government purchasing.

Appendix

References
and Sources

One of the main and most important keys to commanding the best prices for what you offer is to have enough avenues of new business so that you can operate with a solid sense of independence and not of desperation or of being an underdog. Having access to a multiplicity of business aids and assets therefore itself multiplies your leverage—your strength in pricing. Providing you that multiplicity of aids and assets is the main objective of this final section, an appendix of useful information.

There are many sources of information and help, direct and indirect, that you can turn to to learn what going rates are in various businesses and localities. Even when you know or think you know all that there is to know about your industry and your market, changes are taking place constantly, and it is never easy to know what is true at the moment. When I was assured that the post-Christmas season—January and February—were among the worst of months for doing business, I sometimes found these excellent months for business. But not in every year: In some years, they were indeed terrible months for business.

There are many truths about business, as about other things, but they are only today's truths. Tomorrow's truths may be far dif-

ferent. One needs to have some means for assessing truth con-
tinuously, almost on a daily basis.

It is for that reason, among others, that I have my name on
many subscription lists and distribution lists, including many on
the Internet, on CompuServe, on popular magazines and on others.
Just this morning, as I write this, I received a press release from
NATSS, the National Association of Temporary and Staffing Services, reporting on the state of that industry, with several charts
and tables to illustrate their points. (They are at 119 S. St. Asaph
Street. Alexandria, VA 22314, 703-549-6287, ext. 118.)

What follows are references that have been of use to me. And
I happen to think—and hope—that they may be of use to you also.
Choose from among them whatever you think will help you conduct your own business in such a way as to command the best possible prices for the best possible service.

U.S. Small Business Administration

The U.S. Small Business Administration (SBA) operates nearly
100 offices in the United States and possessions. SBA offers a number of helpful services to small businesses, including consulting
and counseling services of various kinds. Any given SBA office can
guide you with respect to local business conditions, for example.

Following is a listing to help you find the nearest SBA office
in your own service area:

Alabama
Birmingham 35205
908 S. 20th Street, Room 202

Alaska
Anchorage 99501
1016 W. 6th Avenue, Suite 200

Fairbanks 99701
Federal Building & Courthouse
   Street

Arizona
Phoenix 85004
112 N. Central Avenue

Arkansas
Little Rock 72202
611 Gaines Street, Suite 900

California
Fresno 93721
1229 N Street

Los Angeles 90071
360 S. Figueroa Street

Sacramento 95825
2800 Cottage Way, Room 2535

San Diego 92188
880 Front Street, Room 4-S-38

San Francisco 94102
450 Golden Gate Avenue

211 Main Street, 4th Floor

Colorado
Denver 80202
1405 Curtis Street, 22nd Floor

721 19th Street

Connecticut
Hartford 06103
1 Financial Plaza

Delaware
Wilmington 19801
844 King Street, Room 5207

District of Columbia
Washington 20416
1441 L Street, NW

Washington 20417
1030 15th Street, NW

Florida
Coral Gables 33134
2222 Ponce de Leon Boulevard

Jacksonville 32202
400 West Bay Street, Room 261

Tampa 33607
700 Twiggs Street

West Palm Beach 33402
701 Clematis Street

Georgia
Atlanta 30309
1375 Peachtree Street, NW

Guam
Agana 96910
Pacific Daily News Building

Hawaii
Honolulu 96850
300 Ala Moana, Box 50207

Idaho
Boise 83702
1005 Main Street

Illinois
Chicago 60604
219 South Dearborn Street

Springfield 62701
1 North Old State Capital Plaza

Indiana
Indianapolis 46204
575 N. Pennsylvania Street

Iowa
Des Moines 50309
210 Walnut Street, Room 749

Kansas
Wichita 67202
110 East Waterman Street

Kentucky
Louisville 40202
600 Federal Plaza, Room 188

Louisiana
New Orleans 70113
1001 Howard Avenue, 17th Floor

Shreveport 71101
500 Fannin Street

Maine
Augusta 04330
40 Western Avenue, Room 512

Maryland
Baltimore/Towson 21204
LaSalle Road

Massachusetts
Boston 02114
60 Batterymarch, 10th Floor

Holyoke 01050
302 High Street, 4th Floor

Michigan
Detroit 48226
477 Michigan Avenue

Marquette 49855
540 West Kave Avenue

Minnesota
Minneapolis 55402
12 South 6th Street

Mississippi
Biloxi 39530
111 Fred Haise Boulevard

Jackson 39201
200 East Pascagoula Street

Missouri
Kansas City 64106
911 Walnut Street, 23rd Floor

1150 Grande Avenue

St. Louis 63101
1 Mercantile Center

Montana
Helena 59601
301 South Park, Drawer 10054

Nebraska
Omaha 68102
Empire State Bldg., 2nd Floor

Nevada
Las Vegas 89101
301 East Stewart Street

Reno 89505
50 South Virginia Street,
  Room 213

New Hampshire
Concord 03301
55 Pleasant Street, Room 213

New Jersey
Camden 08104
1800 East Davis Street

Newark 07102
970 Broad Street, Room 1635

New Mexico
Albuquerque 87110
5000 Marble Avenue, NE

New York
Albany 12210
99 Washington Avenue, Room
  301

North Carolina
Charlotte 28202
230 South Tryon Street

Greenville 27834
215 South Evans Street, Room
  206

North Dakota
Fargo 58102
65 72nd Avenue North, Room
  218

Ohio
Cincinnati 45202
550 Main Street, Room 5028

Cleveland 44199
1240 East 9th Street, Room 317

Columbus 43215
85 Marconi Boulevard

Oklahoma
Oklahoma City 73102
200 NW 5th Street, Room 670

Oregon
Portland 97205
1220 SW 3rd Avenue, Federal
  Building

Pennsylvania
Harrisburg 17101
100 Chestnut Street

Philadelphia/Bala-Cynwyd 19004
1 Bala-Cynwyd Plaza

Pittsburgh 15222
1000 Liberty Avenue, Room 1401

Wilkes-Barre 18702
20 N. Pennsylvania Avenue

Puerto Rico
Hato Rey 00919
Chardon and Bolivia Streets

Rhode Island
Providence 02903
40 Fountain Street

South Carolina
Columbia 29201
1801 Assembly Street, Room 131

South Dakota
Rapid City 57701
515 9th Street, Room 246

Sioux Falls 57102
101 S. Maine Avenue

Tennessee
Knoxville 37902
502 S. Gay Street, Room 307

Memphis 38103
167 N. Main Street, Room 211

Nashville 37219
404 James Robertson Parkway

Texas
Corpus Christi 78408
3105 Leopard Street

Dallas 75202
1100 Commerce Street, Room
  3C36

Dallas 75235
1720 Regal Row, Room 230

El Paso 79901
4100 Rio Bravo, Suite 300

Harlingen 78550
222 E. Van Buren Street

Houston 77002
500 Dallas Street

1 Allen Center

Lubbock 79401
1205 Texas Avenue, Room 712

Marshall 75670
100 South Washington Street

San Antonio 78206
727 East Durango, Room A-513

Utah
Salt Lake City 84138
125 South State Street

Vermont
Montpelier 06502

Virginia
Richmond 23240
400 N. 8th Street, Room 3015

Virgin Islands
St. Thomas 00801
Veterans Drive, U.S. Federal
  Building

Washington
Seattle 98104
710 2nd Avenue, 5th Floor

915 2nd Avenue, Room 1744

Spokane 99210
Court House Building, Room 651

West Virginia
Charleston 25301
Charleston National Plaza

Clarksburg 26301
109 N. 3rd Street

Wisconsin
Eau Claire 54701
500 S. Barstow Street

Madison 53703
212 E. Washington Avenue

Wyoming
Casper 82602
100 East B. Street

State Programs

Although the U.S. Small Business Administration operates the most
ambitious slate of business-assistance programs, many of the states

operate their own programs to support businesses, especially small businesses. These programs fall generally into five categories:

- Loans and loan guarantees
- Consulting/counseling and administrative services
- Preferences (extra points awarded) in procurement
- Handling and adjusting complaints of various kinds
- Legislative activity in enacting legislation for future programs

Following is a starter list of known offices and programs. This list may not be complete, however, and it is a good idea to check in your own state. Make inquiry of your own state's purchasing and supply agency. They will know of any state programs regarding the support of business in doing business in the state.

Alabama

Alabama gives preference for a small business, defined in Alabama as one with fewer than 50 employees or less than $1 million in gross annual receipts. The Department of Industrial Relations is authorized to render a variety of services to help small businesses win state contracts. Contact the Office of State Planning, 3734 Atlanta Highway, Montgomery, AL 36130.

Alaska

Alaska has several loan programs, all of them rather comprehensive and well defined, that include both direct loans from the state and bank-participation loans, wherein the state and the bank are colenders. Alaska also operates a small business assistance office. Contact the Division of Economic Enterprise, Department of Commerce and Economic Development, 675 7th Avenue, Station A, Fairbanks, AK 99701.

Arizona

Little information on Arizona's socioeconomic programs is available at this moment. Contact Arizona's Office of Economic Planning and Development, 1700 West Washington, Room 400, Phoenix, AZ 85007.

Arkansas

Arkansas has established a small business office. Contact Arkansas's Small Business Assistance Division, Arkansas Department of Economic Development, One State Capitol Mall, Little Rock, AR 72201.

California

California offers a comprehensive set of socioeconomic programs, including loan programs and a Small Business Procurement Office to give procurement preference to small business in the state. Requirements are that the business be located in California and not dominant in the relevant industry, to qualify for such preference. (Of course, you may always bid for state contracts without qualifying for preference.) Contact the Small Business Procurement Office, Department of General Services, 1823 14th Street, Sacramento, CA 95807.

Colorado

Colorado has a Small Business Council and also provides a number of other services to small business. Contact The Small Business Assistance Center, University of Colorado, Campus Box 434, Boulder, CO 80309; and the Colorado Department of Local Affairs, Division of Commerce and Development, 1313 Sherman Street, Room 500, Denver, CO 80203.

Connecticut

Connecticut has a definite small-business set-aside requirement and defines small businesses as those that have been domiciled and doing business in the state for at least one year and whose annual revenues are not in excess of $1 million for the previous fiscal year. Contact the Office of Small Business Affairs, Department of Economic Development, State Office Building, Hartford, CT 06115.

Florida

Contact the Office of Business Assistance, Executive Office of the Governor, Tallahassee, FL 32301.

Georgia

Georgia defines small business as having fewer than 100 employees or less than $1 million in gross annual receipts. An advisory council of small business representatives offers counsel on procurement matters to Georgia's Department of Administrative Services.

Hawaii

Hawaii uses the federal (SBA) definition of small business as their own and operates a loan program also. Contact the Department of Planning and Economic Development, 250 South King Street, Honolulu, HI 96813.

Illinois

Illinois has a Department of Commerce and Community Affairs within which is included the Illinois Office of Business Services.

This office incorporates the duties and services formerly provided by the old Small Business Information Office. Contact the Illinois Office of Business Services, 180 North LaSalle Street, Chicago, IL 60701; and/or the Small Business Coordinator, Department of Administrative Services, Stratton Office Building, Room 802, Springfield, IL 62707.

Indiana

Indiana now has a Small Business Ombudsman office to help small business in a variety of ways, including help in bidding for state contracts. Contact the Ombudsman Office, 503 State Office Building, Indianapolis, IN 46204.

Iowa

Iowa operates an Office of Ombudsman and a legislative program for small business. Address inquiries to Iowa Citizens' Aide Office, State Capitol, Des Moines, IA 50319.

Kansas

Kansas establishes as a goal the setting aside for small business of at least 10 percent of state purchases and has a legislative program as well. Among several other criteria, businesses must meet standards of numbers of employees and/or annual dollar volume set for different industries to qualify as small business in the state.

Kentucky

Kentucky has a small business office to oversee and manage its small business programs, which includes small business set-asides in state procurement. Contact the Small Business Development

Section, Small and Minority Business Development Division, Kentucky Department of Commerce, Capital Plaza, Frankfort, KY 40601.

Louisiana

Louisiana has a small business set-aside program and defines small business according to standards of numbers of employees and annual volume, which vary for different types of enterprises. Contact the Louisiana Department of Commerce, Office of Commerce and Industry, POB 44185, Baton Rouge, LA 70804.

Maine

Contact the Maine Development Foundation, One Memorial Circle, Augusta, ME 04333.

Maryland

In-state small businesses in Maryland get a 5 percent preference over out-of-state bidders for state contracts. Contact the Office of Business Liaison and the Office of Business and Industrial Development, Department of Economic and Community Development, 1748 Forest Drive, Annapolis, MD 21401. An Office of Minority Business Enterprise is located at the same address.

Massachusetts

Massachusetts operates a broad spread of small business programs and other programs for business generally, including general assistance to small business in winning both state and federal contracts and offering an extensive consultative assistance. Contact the Division of Small Business Assistance, Department of Commerce and Development, 100 Cambridge Street, Boston, MA 02202. Also contact the Business Information Center/Network (BIC/NET) and Business Service Center within the same Department and at the same address. Also Massachusetts Technology Development Corporation, 131 State Street, Boston, MA 02109 and Massachusetts Business Development Corporation, One Boston Place, Boston, MA 02108.

Michigan

Michigan offers a variety of business-assistance programs, including help in winning state contracts. For small and minority business assistance programs contact the Business Enterprise Specialist, Purchasing Division, Department of Management and Budget, Mason Building, 2nd Floor, Lansing, MI 48909; and the Small Business Development Division, Office of Economic Development, Michigan Department of Commerce, POB 30225, Lansing, MI 48909.

Minnesota

Minnesota has as a goal the awarding of 20 percent of the state's procurement dollars to small business, defined as one with not more than 20 employees nor more than $1 million in annual revenues. The program is administered by the Department of Economic Development, 480 Cedar Street, St. Paul, MN 55101.

Mississippi

Mississippi operates a broad spread of programs for small business, including publications, consultation, training and procurement preference, and has a number of offices with related functions in different areas of the state. Contact the Small Business Assistance Division, Agricultural and Industrial Board, Agriculture and

Commerce Department, 301 Walter Sillers Building, Jackson, MS 39205.

Missouri

Little information is available currently about Missouri's small business programs (relevant legislation was pending at the time of this writing), but the state advises that small businesses should seek assistance from the program of Existing Business Assistance, Division of Community and Economic Development, Jefferson City, MO 65102.

Montana

Montana includes within its small business programs one that pledges that "all agencies will ensure that a fair proportion of the state government's total purchases and contracts for property and services are placed with small business concerns." Contact the Office of Commerce and Small Business Development, Governor's Office, Room 212, Capitol Station, Helena, MT 59601.

New Jersey

New Jersey has a small business assistance office with a rather general and broadly defined mission to aid small business. Contact the New Jersey Department of Labor and Industry, John Fitch Plaza, Trenton, NJ 08625.

New Mexico

New Mexico has no specific program for small business, but vendors are invited to contact the Existing Industry Liaison, Economic Development Division, Santa Fe, NM 85703.

New York

New York's several small business programs include one offering help in winning state contracts. Contact the Division of Ombudsmen and Small Business Services, 230 Park Avenue, New York, NY 10017.

North Carolina

North Carolina has a small business program but without any specific dollar or percentage goals. Contact the Business Assistance Division, North Carolina Department of Commerce, 430 North Salisbury Street, Raleigh, NC 27611.

Ohio

Contact the Office of Small Business Assistance, Ohio Department of Economic and Community Development, Columbus, OH 43215.

Oregon

Contact the Small Business Office, Director for Business/Government Relations, Department of Economic Development, Salem, OR 97310.

Pennsylvania

Pennsylvania does not have a special small business program but takes the position that all businesses should have all possible assistance and services from the state. There is, however, a Small Business Service Center, South Office Building, Room G-13, Harrisburg, PA 17120.

Tennessee

Contact the Small Business Information Center, Department of Economic & Community Development, 107 Andrew Jackson State Office Building, Nashville, TN 37219.

Texas

Texas has a small business procurement program, among others, which has the goal of awarding at least 10 percent of the state's procurement dollars to small business, defined as those with fewer than 100 employees or less than $1 million in annual revenues. Contact the Purchasing and General Services Commission, 1711 San Jacinto Street, Austin, TX 78701.

Utah

Utah has a small business office. Contact the Business Development Coordinator, No. 2 Arrow Press Square, Suite 260, 165 South West Temple, Salt Lake City, UT 84101.

Vermont

Contact the Vermont Economic Opportunity Office, Montpelier, VT 05602.

West Virginia

West Virginia sets general goals for awards to small business, defined by using federal SBA standards. Contact the Small Business Service Unit, Governor's Office of Economic and Community Development, Building 6, Suite B-564, Capitol Complex, Charleston, WV 25305.

Wisconsin

Wisconsin includes a small business procurement program. Contact the Small Business Ombudsman, Department of Business Development, Madison, WI 53702.

Local Government Programs

Many local governments—those of counties, cities, towns and townships—operate programs of preference for and general assistance to small business and minority enterprises. Purchasing officers should know of any such programs, and inquiry should be made of the purchasing offices in these jurisdictions to ensure that you learn of and can take advantage of such programs for which you qualify.

Small Business Development Centers

The SBA is not alone in its endeavors on behalf of small business. SBA and the state governments fund hundreds of Small Business Development Centers throughout the country, many of them in universities and colleges. These provide a variety of services to small business, including seminars, counseling and other functions. Check with your nearest SBA office for the location of the nearest Small Business Development Center.

Online Assistance

The steadily growing wealth of online facilities and services offers a great deal of help. CompuServe, GEnie, America Online and other such services offer daily contact with thousands of individuals who report their own opinions and experiences as independent practitioners of various kinds. Many include extensive libraries of information you may download to your own computer, including schedules of rates. Here is a short starter list of the best known of these online utilities.

Online Utilities

CompuServe
5000 Arlington Center Boulevard
Columbus, OH 43220
617-457-8600
800-848-8990

America Online
8619 Westwood Center Drive
Falls Church, VA
703-893-6288
800-827-6364

GEnie
401 N. Washington Street
Rockville, MD 20850
301-340-4000
800-638-9636

The Internet

The Internet is referred to sometimes as the "Information Super-highway." It merits that designation: The current resources available on "the Net" are truly staggering, and the potential for the future even more so. Here are just a few of the many localities on the Net where you may find information relevant to what we have discussed in these pages:

The Catalog of Federal Domestic Assistance is a government publication that lists and describes a great many government programs, many of them grant programs, but many provide assistance to small business in various ways, at low and no cost. These include counseling services, publications and preference programs. The catalog may be purchased in printed form from the U.S. Government Printing Office bookstores or on disk from the General Services Administration. Information is available on the Internet at the following address:

http://www.sura.net/main/members/gsa.shtml

The catalog may be searched on the Internet by dialing up the following Internet address:

gopher://gopher.sura.net:70/7waissrc:/network.res.gsa-cfda

Information on government procurement of goods and services is available in the *Consumer Information Catalog, Doing Business with GSA.* On the Internet, enter the following address:

http://www.gsa.gov/gsapubs.htm

A number of reports and explanations about state government procurement are available to read, download or print out at the following Internet addresses:

http://www.csus.edu.procure.html
http://www.infoseek.com/Titles?qt=state+government
+procurement

Government Bulletin Boards

The SBA electronic bulletin board provides a gateway to many other government bulletin boards and to the Internet itself. If you are in the Washington, DC, metropolitan area, call the board on 202-401-9600 and get maximum access to all facilities, including a gateway to a great many other government bulletin boards. Otherwise, you can ring up the SBA on a toll-free line at 1-800-697-4636. Your access will be somewhat limited there, but the SBA will then provide you a 900 number that offers complete access.

A Few "Going Rates"

Following are suggested market rates for various skills, crafts and functions suggested by a number of writers. Obviously, they range over a spectrum, and there are no doubt a great many exceptions to these suggested rates. Many individuals will provide services at more modest rates, while there are always some who charge and get much higher rates. A good copywriter might be available for less than $100 per hour, for example, but there are some especially effective copywriters who charge and get many hundreds of dollars per hour for their services. That is true for many specialties, especially for those which call for creativity, great skill or technical knowledge. But it is also true for those who have great marketing skill, as discussed earlier in these pages. These rates are therefore offered primarily to help your thinking as to the "ballpark" for average practitioners in most of the areas referred to.

The same considerations apply to the suggested flat rates that follow. Many resume writers will turn out a one- or two-page resume for $30 to $50, but there are others whose prices start at $100 or more, minimum, for even a one-page resume. Brochures, sales letters and other items are similarly highly variable in both size and difficulty of writing and composing. The word "brochure" is a highly variable one, of course, as was noted in discussing the subject in an earlier chapter.

It probably should be noted here that with today's small-office equipment—computers, laser printers and highly sophisticated software—many entrepreneurs who offer such services as copywriting include composition of the product in their price, and they deliver camera-ready copy to the customer. However, there are customers who have their own final copy and want only composition or other desktop publishing services, so it is necessary to have separate rates for desktop publishing.

Hourly Rates for Service Professionals

Accountants:	$60–$150
Bookkeepers:	$25–$40
Commercial artists:	$45–$125
Computer specialists:	$40–$75
Consulting:	$60–$150
Copywriters:	$40–$100
Desktop publishing	$35–$75
Newsletter writing:	$40–$100

Public relations:	$75–$125
Technical writing:	$40–$90
Trainers:	$35–$60
Writing, general:	$40–$75

Flat Rates for Typical Services

Brochure, writing:	$200 up
Brochure, composing:	$75 up
Direct mail package:	$2,000–$4,000
Newsletter, writing:	$300–$600/page
Press release:	$125–$300/page
Resume, writing:	$35–$65
Resume, composing:	$25–$40
Sales letter:	$300–$1,500

Barter Exchanges

Itex of Denver
13741 East Rice Place, Suite 106
Aurora, CO 80015
303-699-0644

American Trade Association
PO Box 285
San Rafael, CA 92702
415-883-3242

Enterprise Marketing
57 E. 11th Street
New York, NY 10003
212-260-7200

Trade American Card
777 South Main Street, Suite #77
Orange, CA 92668
714-543-8283

Trade Services Int'l
5350 Commerce Blvd, Suite C
Rohnert Park, CA 94928
707-585-7722

Hawaii Barter Exchange
582 Folsom Street
San Francisco, CA 94105
415-777-0123

Internet Business Network
5455 Garden Grove Blvd, Suite 160
Westminister, CA 92683
714-898-5654

New Orleans Trade Exchange
PO Box 19181
New Orleans, LA 70179
504-486-9500

Genesis International Ltd.
2 Lafayette Court
Greenwich, CT 06830
203-629-3355

Butcher Trade Exchange, Inc.
P.O. Box 57
Fort Washington, PA 19034
800-523-5990

**Continental Resource Mktg
   Inc.**
7601 Della Drive, Suite 274
Orlando, FL 32819
407-345-0052

Buyers Business Network
95 Main Street
Maynard, MA 01754
508-461-5100

Island Wide Marketing, Inc.
7A Main Street
Kings Park, NY 11754
516-269-0700

The Trade Exchange, Inc.
2 Gorham Road, Box 2
Scarborough, ME 04074
800-734-0734

American Barter Exchange
585 Stewart Avenue
Garden City, NY 11530
516-222-2495

Barter Plus, Inc.
P.O. Box 2401
Sarasota, FL 34230
813-755-4224

NCE Long Island
400 Jericho Turnpike
Jericho, NY 11753
516-935-2280

Bartermax, Inc.
P.O. Box 415
Sharon, MA 02067
617-769-3400

Bettercard of Little Rock
P.O. Box 21408
Little Rock, AR 72221
501-376-2278

Barter USA
3371 Bayshore Drive
Naples, FL 33962
813-775-9111

Business Exchange Int'l
131 Tustin Avenue, Suite 210
Tustin, CA 92681
714-973-1712

Exchange Enterprises Ltd.
50 Washington Street
So. Norwalk, CT 06854
203-866-8848

The Exchange
5072 Edgewater Drive
Orlando, FL 32810
305-291-2952

**American Commerce
   Exchange**
10556 Riverside Drive
Toluca Lake, CA 91602
818-769-2223

International Barter Exchange
4000 S. Tamiami Trail, Suite 408
Sarasota, FL 34231
800-881-2262

Albert Associated
85-65 130 Street, PO Box "P"
Kew Gardens, NY 11415
718-805-0128

The Itex Corporation
9790 SW Pembrook Street
Portland, OR 97224
503-684-6105

NCE of Tampa Bay, Inc.
14011 66th Street North
Largo, FL 34641
813-229-0729

Trade Works, Inc.
187 Columbia Turnpike, Suite F
Florham Park, NJ 07932
201-538-5566

Cleveland Trade Network, Inc.
24601 Center Ridge Road, Suite 200
Westlake, OH 44145
216-835-0550

Chicago Barter Corp.
18W100 22nd Street, Suite 100
Oakbrook Terrace, IL 60521
708-955-8100

NCE of St. Louis
106 Four Seasons Center, Suite 107B
St. Louis, MO
314-469-1919

Michigan Trade Exchange, Inc.
23200 Coolidge Highway
Oak Park, MI 48237
313-544-1350

TradeCard, Inc.
707 Enterprise Drive
Westerville, OH 43081
614-846-4041

NCE of Charleston
2331 Technical Pkwy, Suite C
N. Charleston, SC 29418
803-824-1435

Bottom Line Business Exchange
50 Northwestern Drive, Suite #9
Salem, NH 03079
603-890-3818

Texas Area Barter Service
21-A Kengle Drive
Arden, NC 28704
704-255-0981

Banc Marc
8001 Franklin Farms Drive
Richmond, VA 23229
804-285-2554

Illinois Trade Association
4208 Commercial Way
Glenview, IL 60025
708-390-6000

Barter Systems Intl
4254 Gate Crest
San Antonio, TX 78217
512-650-9300

Barter Network, Inc.
53 River Street
Milford, CT 06460
203-874-8962

Bus & Prof Trade Exchange
143 E. Shaker Road
P.O. Box 68
E. Longmeadow, MA 01106
617-732-7229

BXI Northeast Alabama
Thomas Shanklin
205-635-0007

BXI Alaska
Jerry "JK" Kemnitz
907-562-2925

BXI Phoenix
Lee & Terry Brandfass
602-951-2929

BXI Tucson
Lee & Terry Brandfass
602-951-2929

BXI Northwest Arkansas
Mary Hallgren
501-443-0255

BXI West Los Angeles
Alan Zimmelman
213-935-2929

**BXI East Los Angeles/
   Hispanic**
Daniel Correa
Esperanza Ayuso
310-649-4905

BXI East San Fernando Valley
Martin Nobler
818-506-2929

**BXI West San Fernando
   Valley**
Jym Mercado
818-703-8331

**BXI Antelope Valley/Santa
   Clarita**
Jym Mercado
805-273-5561

BXI Ventura/Santa Barbara
Diane Van Trees
805-339-0522

BXI Downey/Long Beach
Robert Simpson
310-804-0577

BXI South Bay
Robert Simpson
310-804-0577

BXI Inland Valley
Peter Brooks
909-592-7727

BXI Pasadena/Glendale
Jim Munson
818-449-6124

BXI High Desert
Sam & Cathy Vizzinni
619-949-3800

BXI Coachella Valley
Ron Cleary
619-320-7748

BXI Riverside/San Bernardino
Jeff Sinclair
909-386-5256

BXI Orange County
Ilan Ben-Yosef
714-847-5477

BXI San Diego
Duncan Banner
619-280-2929

BXI San Francisco
Bob Dorentsreich
510-554-3181

BXI San Jose
Stuart Kadas
408-554-1446

BXI Santa Clara County
John Lute
408-297-5532

BXI Oakland/Berkeley/ Fremont
Phil Gill
510-444-4177

BXI Napa
Jim Kisiel
707-252-6214

BXI Marin
Mark Scott, Jr.
415-897-6209

BXI Fresno
Alan Hickman
209-275-6380

BXI Bakersfield
Mark Keyser
209-539-0905

BXI San Francisco Peninsula
Ron Keister
415-761-9300

BXI Monterey/Carmel/Santa Cruz
Nico Bishoff
408-372-7247

BXI Concord/Pleasanton/ Livermore
Doelle Cecaci
510-355-0711

BXI Sacramento
Ron Keister, Len Travis
916-966-8500

BXI Stockton
Al Weist, Shirley Weist
209-464-0294

BXI Sonora
Gregory Slazas
209-533-0626

BXI San Luis Obispo
Kathleen & Mark Goularte
805-481-5980

BXI Colorado
Karl Stout, Bill Cavode
303-694-3236

BXI Connecticut
Roger Boroway, Susan Nadim
203-256-9001

BXI Orlando/Central Florida
Josh Duclos
407-869-7002

BXI South Florida/Boca Raton
Mike Hoffman
407-994-2442

BXI Ft. Lauderdale/Miami
Mike Hoffman
407-994-2442

BXI Broward/Dade Counties
Stanley Cohen
305-565-4900

BXI East Ft. Lauderdale
Mike Hoffman
305-565-4900

BXI Melbourne/Vero Beach
Mike Hoffman
407-728-7772

BXI Merritt Island
Mike Hoffman
407-453-2177

BXI Gainesville
Maria Vakharia
904-462-0687

BXI Atlanta
Jerry Hasty
404-931-4637

BXI Georgia
Frank Scott
404-929-8500

BXI Hawaii
Dr. Gary Ault
808-874-7047

BXI Boise/Southern Idaho
Phil Ingersoll
208-888-0932

BXI Kansas City
Matthew Moots
913-831-3737

BXI Lexington
James Coffman
606-293-6497

BXI Gulf Coast Mississippi
Martin "Mickey" Rehbein
601-374-8182

BXI Montana
Karen Welch
406-849-5472

**BXI Las Vegas/Southern
 Nevada**
Frank Dobrucki
702-798-2933

BXI Reno/Tahoe
Linda Rubendall
702-829-2990

BXI Metropolitan New Jersey
Herb Greenberg
609-497-0880

BXI New Mexico
Terry Brandfass, Todd Aurit
505-298-2929

BXI New York
Yosef Yarmak
212-673-3700

BXI Queens/Brooklyn
Brent Garber
212-260-7200

BXI Eastern New York
Robert Powers
914-934-0731

BXI Raleigh/North Carolina
Ronnie Graham
919-954-1920

BXI Durham/Chapel Hill
Ronnie Graham
919-942-1962

BXI Wilmington/Myrtle
Ronnie Graham
919-452-4161

BXI Charlotte
Doug Barnett, Ronnie Graham
704-525-1617

BXI Cincinnati
Bill LaSelle
513-351-4294

BXI Dayton
Dave Doty
513-259-1058

BXI Columbus
Mark Faber, Kim Spiers
614-848-7788

BXI Oklahoma City
Jack Denny
405-528-2266

BXI Tulsa
Alan Elias, Trish Elias
918-749-2266

BXI Eugene
Cleve Warren
503-343-3365

BXI Portland
Cam Thomas
610-372-1600

BXI Charleston
Michael Saboe
803-762-7144

BXI Memphis
Scott Walker, Stan Rojeski
901-324-8817

BXI Middle & East Tennessee
Pam Duzak
615-298-2161

BXI Dallas
Tom Austin
214-350-6282

BXI Fort Worth/Arlington
Tom Austin
214-350-6282

BXI Houston
Richard Daniels
713-726-0877

BXI Alief/Houston
Larry Kibbee
713-495-7523

BXI Utah
Kirk Dopp
801-561-8402

BXI Southern Utah
Mark and Sarah Jackson
801-635-0521

BXI Seattle
Don Davis
206-885-6675

BXI Spokane/Idaho Panhandle
Rod Bloom
509-924-2043

BXI Vancouver, Washington
Ron Lauser
503-452-4544

BXI Travel/Vacation
Nancy Thiede
714-502-9034

**BXI Special Projects,
Entertainment**
Richard Byard
818-848-4966

Index